M000165837

The Longhaired Cat

Howell Book House

Howell Book House
A Simon & Schuster Macmillan Company
1633 Broadway
New York, NY 10019

Library of Congress Cataloging-in-Publication Data
Sadler, Anna.
The longhaired cat: an owner's guide to a happy, healthy pet / by
Anna Sadler.
p. cm.
Includes bibliographical references.

ISBN 0-87605-476-9 (hardcover)

1. Longhair cats. I. Title.
SF449.L65S34 1996
636.8'3—dc20 96-3951
CIP

Manufactured in the United States of America
10 9 8 7 6 5 4 3 2 1

Series Director: Dominique DeVito
Series Assistant Directors: Ariel Cannon and Sarah Storey
Book Design: Michele Laseau
Cover Design: Iris Jeromnimon
Illustration: Jeff Yesh
Photography:
Cover Photos by Scott McKiernan/Zuma and Mary Bloom
Joan Balzaraini: 48
Mary Bloom: 38, 40, 72
Paulette Braun/Pets by Paulette: 10, 53, 85, 89
Paul Butler: 15, 18, 20, 34, 59, 121, 126, 133
Chanan: 16, 17, 18, 19, 21, 22, 25, 26, 27, 29, 31, 32, 33, 35, 36
Scott McKiernan/Zuma: 8
Renée Stockdale: 12, 37, 42, 43, 58, 60, 67, 70, 73, 74, 75, 79, 80, 81, 82, 86, 92, 94, 95, 98, 99, 101, 103, 110, 112, 113, 117, 118, 129, 130, 136, 137, 142, 146
Judith Strom: 5, 61
Jean Wentworth: 7, 11, 14, 43, 44, 46, 47, 51, 54, 63, 65, 84, 91, 107, 120, 128, 135, 138
Karrin Winter/Dale Churchill: 52, 77, 140
Production Team: Trudy Brown, Jama Carter, Kathleen Caulfield, Trudy Coler, Amy DeAngelis, Matt Hannafin, Vic Peterson, Terri Sheehan and Marvin Van Tiem.

Contents

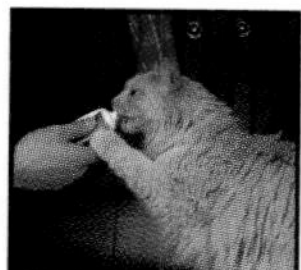

Welcome

to the

World

of the

part one 

Longhaired Cat

External Features of the Longhaired Cat 

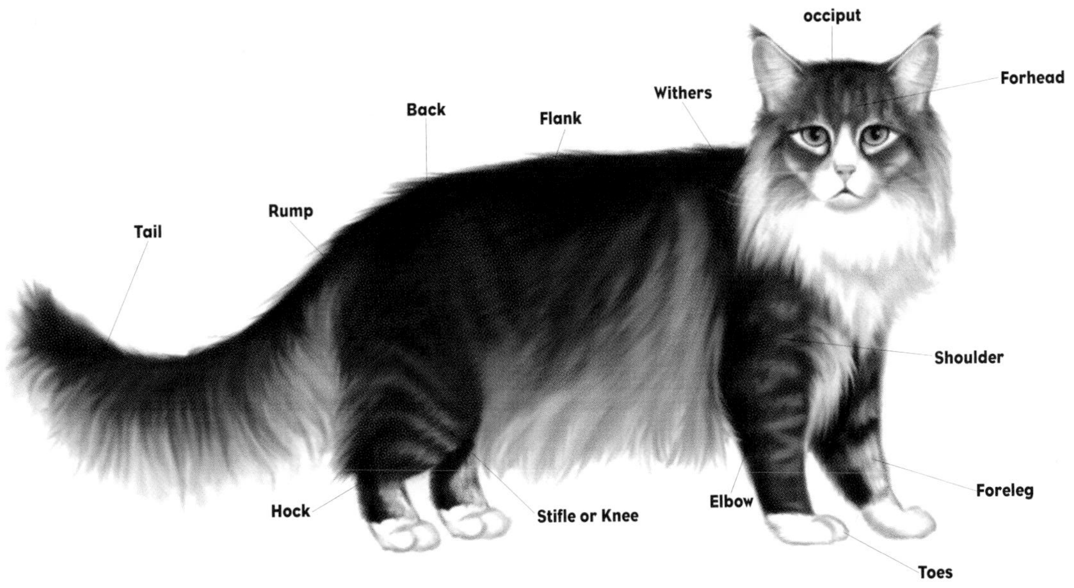

chapter 1

History of the Cat

While evidence of the dog's domestication can be gleaned from anthropological evidence found among the earliest hunter-gatherer cultures some 10,000 to 12,000 years ago, the earliest documented evidence of the cat's interaction with man is not found until about 2000 B.C. in Egypt. Paintings and inscriptions show that cats lived in the homes of Egyptians, and that they were revered, protected and interred in tombs and cemeteries. They were even deified in the cult of the goddess Bast, or Pasht, depicted as a woman with a cat's head. Once the cat's cultural importance was established in

Egypt, the domesticated cat made its way to the Middle East, India, China and finally to Rome.

Rome was the cat's gateway into all of Europe. Prized for their mousing abilities, cats were brought all the way to Scotland and Ireland. Early seafaring explorers carried them on their ships to other parts of the world. While conventional wisdom claims that there were no New World domesticated cats until they sailed with the explorers, some evidence exists in Peruvian art from 1500 B.C. that a smaller, domestic-type cat might have existed there.

Most scholars agree that the origin of today's domestic cat is the African Wild Cat, the *Felis silvestris libyca.* A small, buff-colored cat with darker stripes, it is found throughout Africa and Asia. The evolution of longer coats on cats may have begun when domestic cats mated with the Pallas Cat *(Felis manul)*, a species found in the Caspian sea area and in the steppes of Northern and Central Asia.

Some current cat breeds are now recognized as having longhair variants that began as genetic mutations. The proliferation of these mutations, in combination with the forces of natural selection, created cats in colder climes whose longer, denser coats enabled them to better survive the winter weather.

For centuries the terms "Persian" and "Angora" were virtually interchangeable throughout Europe and America, and the longhaired cat these terms described has been prized for its beauty from the earliest times. Other longhaired breeds developed within

CATS VS. RATS: HOW THE WAR BEGAN

A Madagascan legend tells of how the enmity between cats and rats began. The two once lived in peace, so the story goes, until a famine came over the land and they set out together to find a better life. On their journey, they encountered a river too wide to swim. Together they unearthed a huge yam, and the rat hollowed it out with his teeth to form a canoe. They set off into the river, with the cat paddling. To the cat's dismay, however, the canoe was soon sinking; the rat, due to his ravenous hunger, had begun to eat the edges of the yam, endangering both their lives. Weak and sinking, the rat begged the cat for help. "I will only help you," replied the cat, "if you will allow me to eat you when we reach land." The rat consented, but began planning his escape. When they reached the shore, the rat said, "You must wait to eat me until I am dry, for while I am soggy I will not be good to eat." The cat consented, and the rat used the delay to dig under some tree roots and hide. The cat, hating to be duped, then declared eternal war on all rats; the war continues to this day.

colder geographic regions, probably as descendants of the cats who traveled with early Norse explorers. These new breeds included the Siberian Cat in Russia, the Norwegian Forest Cat in Norway and the Maine Coon Cat in the United States.

One of the oldest longhaired breeds, the Persian has long been prized for its beauty.

Whatever their exact origins, cats have been admired through the centuries for their beauty, grace and independent spirit. They have been valued, from the year 2000 B.C. to today, for their highly efficient predatory instincts. Wherever man has been plagued by rodents, the cat has proved its worth: In the granaries of ancient Egypt, cats could literally mean the difference between plenty and famine; ancient mariners appreciated cats keeping their vessels free of rodents; in the Middle Ages in Europe, cats singlehandedly turned the tide of the rodent-borne bubonic plague; modern ranchers keep barn cats to protect their livestock. In fact, after Hurricane Andrew wiped out entire colonies of feral cats in Florida, a burgeoning population of rats and mice necessitated the introduction of new feral cats to Miami a year later. To date, no one has invented a better mousetrap!

A CAT BY ANY OTHER NAME

In English it's *cat*; in French, *chat*. The Germans call them *Katzen*, the Spanish and Syrians *gatos* and the Arabs *qitt*. The ancient Byzantine word was *katos*, the Latin *catus*. All are from *kadiz*, which was the word for cat in Nubia, an ancient Nile Valley kingdom that included southern Egypt.

Pest Control Through the Ages

Europe was relatively slower than Egypt and Asian countries to recognize the advantages of the domestic cat. Ancient Greece had several small carnivorous animals (the weasel, ermine and stone marten) that controlled rodents that assaulted its granaries; however, these same carnivores were indiscriminate enough to kill chickens, pigeons and even goats. Documentation of when the introduction of cats occurred is sparse; Egypt's prohibition against allowing the Greeks to export cats from Egypt forced the Greeks to carry out clandestine raids to steal them.

Cats, however domesticated these days, still have the mousing skills for which they were first revered.

Plagues are documented from as early as 1070 B.C., when an epidemic broke out. This epidemic, which the Bible called "the plague of the Philistines," killed more than 50,000 people. The Black Death of the mid-1300s claimed twenty-five million lives in Europe and another twenty-three million in Asia, wiping out entire cities and armies. France, South America and India also had massive plagues, all borne by rats. Sooner or later, where there were rats, people came to appreciate cats.

Because of their ratting abilities, cats have literally been the saviour of many civilizations. In France during the eleventh century, cats were so valued that they were listed in wills. In the mid-tenth century, the legal code of Wales included a law fixing the value of a ratting cat, and also penalties and fines for "those who endangered its life, wounded it, or did not care for it properly." The cat's price varied according to whether its ratting abilities had been proven. Upon killing its first mouse, a cat's value doubled. Some were valued on par with a fourteen-day-old foal, a calf of six, months, or a completely weaned pig.

The Cat as Demon

The cat's popularity has gone through periods of decline as well. The pagan cult of Freyia began in Germany in the Middle Ages. This cult, which honored the fecundity of the cat, conducted rituals that featured orgies and bacchanals that the Church set out to decimate. Cats were then subjected to torture and sacrificial burnings. During the period of the Inquisition, men and women throughout Roman Catholic Europe were tortured, burned or hanged for giving care to a sick or wounded cat or for giving one shelter. In the early American colonies, cats were deemed to be witches' familiars and burned along with their owners.

In the late 1700s the brown rat began to displace the black rat throughout Europe, and to stow away on ships bound for other parts of the world. Napoleon, who hated cats, made every effort to find a solution to the problem, including poisons and the newest in trap technology. All failed, and again cats were called upon to perform their greatest service for man.

THE FIRST CAT

There are a number of different legends that explain how cats made their entrance into the world. According to Hebrew folklore, Noah was concerned that rats might be a problem on the ark by eating all the provisions, and prayed to God for help. God responded by causing the lion, who was sleeping, to unleash a giant sneeze from which emerged a little cat.

In an Arabic legend, Noah's sons and daughters are worried about their safety on the ark because of the presence of the lion. Noah prayed to God for help and God afflicted the lion with a fever. But not too much later another dangerous creature emerged: the mouse. Again Noah prayed and this time God caused the lion to sneeze and the cat issued forth.

In a medieval legend the Devil plays a role in the creation of the cat. Trying to copy God and create a man, the Devil manages only to produce a small, pathetic, skinless animal—the cat. St. Peter felt sorry for the creature and gave it a fur coat, which is the cat's only valuable possession. (From *The Quintessential Cat*, by Roberta Altman. New York: Macmillan, 1994.)

At about that same time in America, entire colonies were overrun by a plague of black rats. To meet this challenge, it was decided in 1749 to import domestic cats into America from Europe. The earlier Viking explorers had left behind some of their feline shipmates along the northeastern seaboard, and these forerunners of the Maine Coon cat were flourishing as well.

The Cat as Pet

In the middle of the nineteenth century the modern cat fancy began. As an urban middle class in both Europe and the United States grew, so did the frequency with which cats were kept as pets. With the Industrial Revolution, people were moving to the cities, and they missed the human-animal bond that had been forged for thousands of years on farms. Their growing affluence allowed them to appreciate cats for their companionship as well as their utility in mousing. Longhaired cats in particular were recognized and prized for their beauty.

The birth of the modern cat fancy gave rise to the growing number of cats "living in style."

Even today, though, there exist rodent-borne diseases, as well as barns and alleyways in need of rat patrol; the cat therefore continues his centuries-old war. In these modern days, the role of the cat has changed in society . . . or has it?

Cats in America

Household pets There are three basic types of cats in modern America. The first is the pampered feline that shares our homes and is protected from the rigors of the outside urban world in which diseases, cars and other animals present a constant danger. These beloved pets are treated to products of the multi-billion-dollar pet industry. Cats can sport jeweled collars, sleep in and climb on a whole array of kitty furniture, and eat gourmand treats such as kitty pâté and omelets. There has been a proliferation of "no dogs allowed" veterinary clinics, grooming salons and boarding facilities in which the cat's individual needs are seen to in the grandest style.

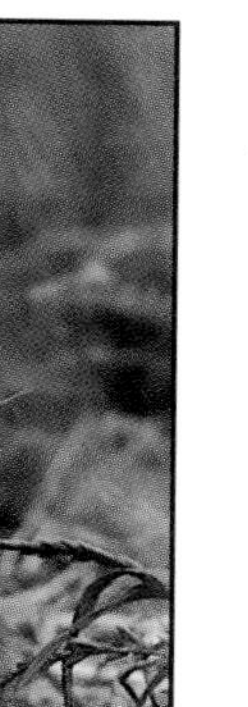

Feral cats are the unfortunate felines forced to survive on resourcefulness and will alone.

During the last decade, the cat has overtaken the dog in numbers, assuming the mantle of "America's Favorite Pet." Cat shows, and the organized cat fancy, have been instrumental in raising the public consciousness of the advantages and joys of owning cats.

Feral cats establish and defend their habitats with fierce territoriality.

Feral cats At the other end of the spectrum, however, is the second type of modern cat, the feral cat. These seemingly wretched creatures can be found eking out an existence from garbage cans in inner-city neighborhoods, behind restaurants in busy downtown areas, on college campuses or in parks in suburbia. Few are found without battle scars, and while the rate of early mortality among these cats is very high, a few streetwise individuals do survive.

Unfortunately, these cats are usually totally untouchable by humans.

Free-roaming cats The third type of modern cat is called the "loosely owned" cat in most jurisdictions. These cats, who probably had owners at one time, have either gotten lost or were abandoned. They may have become semi-feral and reluctant to accept human touch, but have learned the wiles of "begging" for handouts. Most neighborhoods have at least one or two such cats, for whom no one claims actual ownership but who may dine from numerous back porches on the food kind people put out.

Some cats, owned by no one in particular, live on the generosity of a few neighborhood kind-hearted souls.

Kittens born to feral or loosely owned cats face an uncertain future at best. In fact, because they have no owners to get them vaccinated and sterilized, free-roaming and feral cats account for the vast majority of kittens that unfortunately end up in shelters every spring and summer.

Help for Feral Cats

Promising new programs are springing up to aid these cats. After trapping and testing cats for deadly diseases, these benevolent organizations vaccinate and alter the cats, and then release them back into the area where they were originally caught. The theory behind the creation of these programs is proving to be true; feral cats, like other forms of wildlife, establish a territory or "habitat." Population is then controlled by available food, shelter and water within that habitat. Resident cats defend their territory against encroachment by outside cats. However, when cats are trapped and removed permanently, other feral felines simply move into the habitat to fill the void. In TTVAR (Trapped, Tested, Vaccinated, Altered and Released) colonies, the occupancy of a habitat is stabilized; outsider cats are not allowed to move into the territory, and sterilization virtually halts any further reproduction among those cats already present. In most of these TTVAR colonies, animal welfar organizations, cat clubs and neighborhood cat lovers unite to provide the cats with food and water.

Efforts like those demontstrated in the TTVAR projects, in which humans show extraordinary concern for the health and well-being of their feline friends, indicate the extent to which these unique and intriguing creatures are valued in our society. Despite its sometimes maligned existence, the cat has now unquestionably made its way into the hearts and homes of over fifty billion people.

chapter 2

The Longhaired Breeds

For purposes of explaining the longhaired breeds, the reader should first understand their various origins. While the cat fancy is more than a hundred years old, the vast majority of breeds have come into existence only during the last thirty years. Each registry has set rules for the acceptance of new breeds; of concern are whether or not a new breed is distinctive in some way (in color, body type, etc.), whether or not breeding it consistently produces characteristics in keeping with the breed standard, and whether or not a sufficient number of these cats exist to establish a healthy, vigorous gene pool.

Once registration records of these new breeds are begun, a number of these cats must be exhibited in shows as "miscellaneous" or "provisional" breeds, so that judges and other exhibitors can become familiar with them. This process can take many years, and may result in a discrepancy among the different associations concerning a new breed's status or classification.

Longhaired breeds can be divided, for purposes of discussion, among (a) breeds with a well-established history; (b) newer breeds developed by natural selection in various parts of the world and that are now perpetuated by people; (c) breeds originated by crossbreeding established breeds; (d) newly recognized longhair variants of traditional shorthair breeds, where the recessive longhair gene was either introduced by man or is a natural occurrence; and (e) developing breeds, recognized by some associations, and awaiting acceptance by others.

The Persian

The true aristocrat of the cat world, a Persian in full coat and show condition never fails to awe cat show spectators. One of the first breeds to be recognized, today's Persian is descended from a conglomerate of different longhaired cat breeds. Since its recognition as a breed in the mid-nineteenth century, breeders have continually refined and developed the traits that make the Persian unique in the cat world. Its popularity is borne out by its numbers: fully sixty percent of all cats registered with the Cat Fanciers Association are Persian; the remaining forty percent are divided among the thirty-three other breeds. (In CFA, the Himalayan is considered a Persian and is therefore included in that sixty percent; the Himalayan remains a separate breed in other associations.)

Persians

To draw a mental image of the perfect Persian, think round. Everything about the Persian should give the appearance of roundness. The short, or "cobby" body, which is heavily boned, should be complemented by a massive coat. The tail should be short, yet

in proportion to the body. The head is the crowning glory of the Persian, and should be completely round. The face should be framed by an immense ruff, have large round eyes and small rounded ears set low on the head. The short and snub nose should be centered in the face, with a muzzle full and rounded enough to give the appearance of a smile. All of these characteristics combine to create the sweet expression demanded by the Persian standard.

Odd-Eyed White Persian

To facilitate judging, the Persian is broken into seven "divisions" determined by color and pattern. These seven divisions accommodate ninety-seven separate colors or color/pattern combinations!

Shaded Silver Persian

The *Solid Color Division*, usually having the most numerous representatives, includes the dazzling whites. These cats usually have either copper or blue eyes, but some may be odd-eyed, with one copper eye and one blue eye. Other solids include the intense blacks and reds, their paler counterparts in blues and creams, as well as chocolates and lilacs. All of these colors should be sound to the root, without evidence of barring (more than one color on the same piece of hair).

The *Silver and Golden Division* includes the shaded silvers and goldens, both of which boast stunning green eyes. The shading is created by color-tipped ends on a white undercoat. The chinchilla class sports subtle tipping that creates the appearance of a halo of color on both the white-based chinchilla silver and the cream-based chinchilla golden.

The *Smoke and Shaded Division* includes all cats with tipped coats (excluding those which fall into the Silver and Golden division), as well as smokes of all colors. Smokes have the largest amount of tipping; a smoke actually appears to be a solid-colored cat until the hair is parted to reveal the white undercoat. Chinchillas display the least amount of tipping, with what appears to be only a halo of color over a pure white coat. The remaining shaded cats fall between the two extremes of tipping.

Black Smoke Persian

The *Tabby Division* is made up of the classic and mackerel tabbies in all colors. Mackerel tabbies are striped with bands of narrow penciling on the body coat. Classic tabbies have well-defined swirls and bull's-eye–type circles on the sides, and a butterfly marking on the shoulders. Both tabby patterns include necklaces, bracelets, and an "M" marking on the forehead, as well as ringed or barred tails.

Red Classic Tabby Persian

The *Parti-Color Division* is made up of the flashy ladies of the Persians, and is the only division where "no men are allowed." Because of the sex-linked color gene that creates these colors, only females come in tortoiseshell, blue cream, chocolate tortoiseshell and lilac cream.

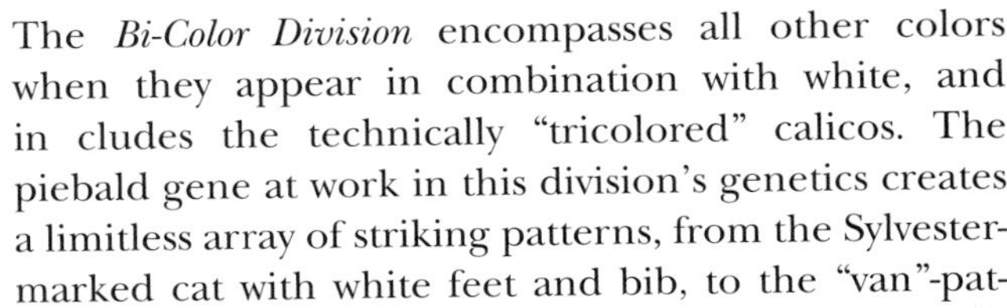

The *Bi-Color Division* encompasses all other colors when they appear in combination with white, and in cludes the technically "tricolored" calicos. The piebald gene at work in this division's genetics creates a limitless array of striking patterns, from the Sylvester-marked cat with white feet and bib, to the "van"-patterned cats, in which the entire cat is white with the exception of color on the head, tail and sometimes the legs.

Dilute Calico Persian

The *Himalayan Division* is still considered a separate breed in many associations. The CFA now considers the Himalayan a Persian, a fact that reflects the many years of dedicated work by breeders who set out to create a cat that has Persian temperament, build and coat, but that also has the color patterning of the Siamese. Himalayan point colors extend beyond the traditional Siamese seal, blue, chocolate and lilac colors, and include such exotic combinations as the seal lynx point (with tabby striping in the point restrictions) or the tortie point (in which the points are a mingling of black and red). In the Himalayan, the body coat color is dependent on the point color, but can range from pure white, to pale ivory, to cream; color is confined to the face, tail and legs.

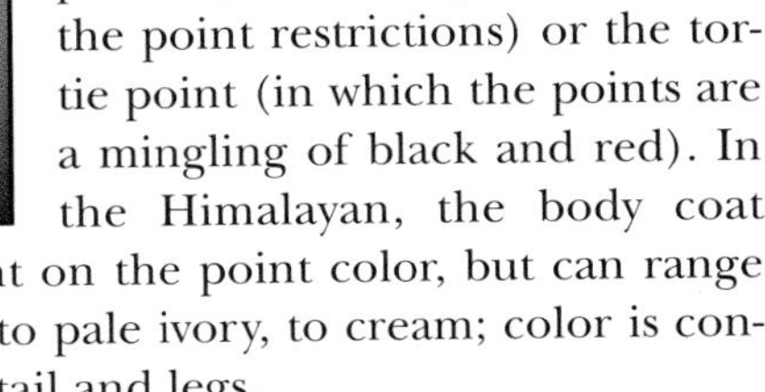

Seal Point Himalayan

Special Persian Features

The Persian has the most gentle, laid-back disposition of all the breeds. While definitely not built for speed or agility, the Persian is still playful and inquisitive. Because it wears a heavy fur coat year-round, the

Persian tends to be warm-natured. Most will seek human laps only for short periods of time, and prefer to lie on cool surfaces somewhere near their human companions. The Persian coat requires a higher level of maintenance than that of any other longhaired breed, but consistent effort pays off as with no other cat; the result is a gorgeous, purring doll-like creature.

Because the Persian is so popular, the breed has been subjected to more misbreeding than any other type of cat. Badly bred cats have led to unfortunate misconceptions about the breed as a whole. For example, many people think of the Persian as an unavoidably sickly cat that is always susceptible to upper respiratory infections because of its short nose. The responsible breeder takes into consideration the fact that humans have intervened to produce a cat that is pleasing to the eye, and therefore pays scrupulous attention to the health of his or her cats. Inbreeding, or any other unhealthy breeding practice, can and does create problems, no matter what the breed. Similarly, careful breeding can produce cats free of these same problems. Even the most "extreme" (flat-faced) Persian can be robust, and never show evidence of breathing problems, dental malocclusion or excessive tearing.

Blue and White Van Persian

Because of the potential problems caused by misbreeding, it is very important, when purchasing a Persian kitten, to see the close relatives of that cat. This kind of visual inspection, in combination with a veterinary examination, is the only way to guarantee that your new cat is free of breeding-related genetic defects.

The Maine Coon

The largest of the longhaired breeds, and ranking second only behind the Persian in popularity, the Maine

Coon is the gentle giant of the cat world. While the Maine Coon is considered a "native" American breed, it was likely introduced by some of the earliest seafaring explorers to land in North America. For this reason, it shares its distant heritage with the other rugged longhaired breeds, the Norwegian Forest Cat and the Siberian Cat.

Maine Coon

The frequently tabby colors of this cat gave rise to a fanciful legend about its origins; the supposed cross-mating between a domestic cat and a raccoon gave this cat its unusual name. The cats roamed the northeastern United States, facing a harsh climate in which only the hardiest could survive. Natural selection ensured that the cat developed into a large, vigorous cat with a dense, water-resistant coat.

Maine Coons have long been a favorite in American show halls, and one received Best in Show at the New York City Cat Show of 1895. With the import of more "exotic" breeds, the Maine Coon diminished in numbers until it was almost extinct in the 1950s. A resurgence in popularity has resulted in large numbers of the breed being shown today.

Adult Maine Coon males usually weigh in at twelve to eighteen pounds, with the females in the ten- to fourteen-pound range. It is a large-boned, broad-chested cat with a long, rectangular body and a long, lavish tail. The coat, the breed's hallmark, comes in the full variety of colors (except point colors), with tabby or tabby and white predominating. The coat varies according to the season: Most of the dense undercoat will be shed during the summer, yet winter attire includes a ruff, foot furnishings (the better to "snow-shoe" with in the Maine woods), ear tufts, and a dense body coat somewhat shorter than the Persian's. The modified wedge-shaped head is broad, and has high, prominent cheekbones, a square muzzle, a slightly concave medium-long nose and a firm chin.

Maine Coons are known for their faithful, loyal and gentle personalities. They are intelligent and inquisitive, very affectionate with their families, yet reserved around strangers.

The Birman

Though documented since before the turn of the century, the emergence of the Sacred Cat of Burma from its homeland was a slow one. According to Birman legend, the original guardians of the Temple of Lao-Tsun were yellow-eyed white cats with long hair. One, named Sinh, was especially devoted to the head priest, Mun-Ha. During an attack on the temple, Mun-Ha was killed; at the moment of his death, Sinh put his feet on his master and turned to the goddess. The cat was transformed: His white fur took on a golden cast, the eyes became as blue as the eyes of the goddess and the face, legs and tail became the color of earth. Only Sinh's paws, where they touched the priest, remained white, as a symbol of purity. All of the other temple cats were transformed as well. Seven days later Sinh died, taking the soul of Mun-Ha to paradise.

Birman

What may have been the original pair of Birmans were clandestinely shipped into France around 1919, leading to the French cat registry's recognition of the breed in 1925. At the end of World War II only two Birmans remained alive in Europe, the outcrossing of which was responsible for the perpetuation of the breed. Eventually the breed crossed the Atlantic, and the Cat Fanciers Association recognized the Birman in 1967.

The Birman is a large, long, stocky cat with long, silky hair that is less dense than a Persian's, and therefore less likely to mat. Point colors are allowed in seal, blue, chocolate and lilac in the CFA, yet breeders across the world are introducing a variety of new point colors not yet accepted in all associations. The eyes are blue and almost round. The face has heavy jaws, a full chin and a Roman nose. Ideally, the white gloves on the front feet are symmetrical with lacing on the rear feet.

While the Birman is gentle, active and playful, his quietness and unobtrusiveness reflect his temple cat heritage.

Turkish Angora

The Turkish Angora

Once thought to be extinct, and still one of the rarer longhaired breeds, the Turkish Angora has reemerged in show halls in recent years. The Turkish Angora is recognized as a pure natural breed that probably originated from the Manul cat domesticated by the Tartars and the Chinese. The breed was further developed in the area of Ankara, Turkey and could be as much as a thousand years old. In fact, prior to the 1880s, they were called Ankara cats because of these origins. The uniqueness of the breed was almost lost, however, as it was bred interchangeably with the Russian Longhair and the Persian. In fact, all three were simply known collectively as "Longhairs."

Happily, though, a controlled breeding program of the Turkish Angora was discovered in Turkey's Ankara Zoo. This fact came to light in 1962, though the zoo's breeding program had been in existence for some forty-five years at that time. A few rare exports from the zoo allowed the reemergence of the Turkish Angora as a breed, and it was accepted for championship status in the Cat Fanciers Association in 1973.

As with many cat breeds, legend abounds regarding the Turkish Angora. The prophet Muhammad was said to have owned a Turkish Angora as a faithful companion. It is said that rather than disturb his feline friend as it slept on his robe, he instead cut off the sleeve.

While the Turkish Angora comes in a full spectrum of colors, the most frequently seen examples are white. The breed is most frequently described as graceful, lithe and limber. They have been referred to as the ballet dancers of the cat world, and as poetry in motion. This small to medium-size cat should be long and fine boned, with large, almond-shaped eyes on a slight upward slant. The head is wedge shaped, with a taper toward the chin, and is topped with wide-set, erect ears that are long, pointed and tufted. The Turkish Angora's unique coat was so prized that it almost led to its extinction. This beautiful coat should be medium long, with a silky texture that tends to wave. It should have a long ruff and a full, bushy tail. There should be no downy undercoat, and a summer shed makes the cat appear almost shorthaired.

Good natured but determined, the Turkish Angora is mischievous, active and prone to vocal and active discussions with his owner. Depend on this cat to state his opinion about virtually everything.

The Somali

A recent surge in public recognition and popularity of this enchanting breed is likely attributable to the *Star Trek* series. The character Data has a Somali. Its foxlike appearance, natural curiosity and easy trainability makes this breed a star in homes, as well as on television.

Among litters since the beginnings of the Abyssinian breed, an occasional longhaired kitten would appear. Since a longhaired coat can be caused by either a recessive gene or a natural mutation from a shorthair coat, the Abyssinian breeders simply shrugged and placed these kittens to be neuters or spays. In the late 1960s and early 1970s, some breeders decided that this longhaired version of the Abyssinian was beautiful in its own right, and deserved a place in show halls as well as pet homes. Abyssinian breeders were opposed to the idea of recognizing a longhaired variant of their breed. Therefore, one of the earliest breeders of this longharied variant, Evelyn Mague, chose to give it the name Somali. (Somalia borders Ethiopia, which was once called Abyssinia.) The Somali Cat Club was founded by Mague in 1972, and breeders began working to have these cats recognized as a separate breed from the parent breed. In a remarkably short period of time this was accomplished, and the CFA recognized the Somali in 1979.

The Somali has many features in common with the Abyssinian, where both temperament and appearance are concerned. The Somali is a medium-long, lithe cat whose rounded rib cage and slightly arched back give it the appearance of a cat about to spring. The head is a slightly rounded wedge; it has gentle contours at the brow, cheek and profile; and it is topped by large, alert ears that are moderately pointed and cupped at the base. The expressive gold or green eyes are almond shaped.

The coat of the Somali is also painted in the parent breed's colors; the CFA allows both ruddy and red, as well as the rarer fawn and blue. Other colors are currently accepted or under consideration by other associations. The medium-length coat is double, giving it a soft and fine, yet dense, feel. A ruff and breeches are preferred. Because of its body style, the Somali is judged in the Shorthair Specialty division of cat shows.

Somali

The Somali is in perpetual motion when awake, and has an abundance of curiosity. Breeders say that they have resilient personalities, adapt easily to new people and homes and adjust well to dogs and other pets. The Somali never walks when she can run, and frequently seeks a soft human lap for a long nap when tired.

The Norwegian Forest Cat

Even the casual cat show visitor should be able to detect the similarities of the Norwegian Forest Cat to its likely distant kin, the Maine Coon. In fact, those similarities probably account for the slow-to-come recognition of the breed in United States cat registries, which demand that new breeds be quite distinctive. Long a favorite in European cat shows, the Norwegian Forest Cat was not accepted by the U.S. fancy until 1984, when the International Cat Association recognized it. The CFA accepted the breed in 1993. The differences between the breeds are distinct but subtle.

The Norwegian Forest Cats are domestic cats evolved in Northern Europe from the earliest cats brought into

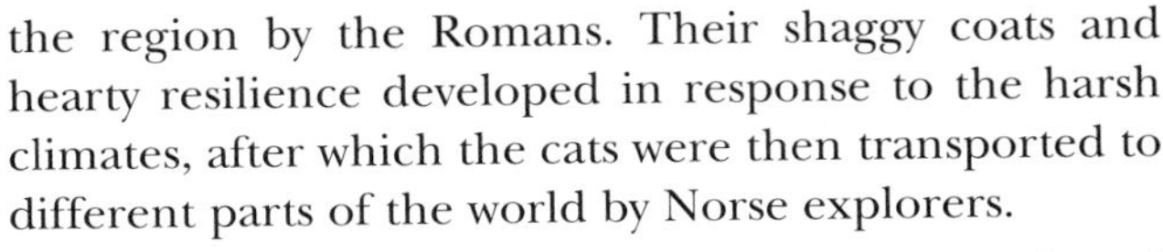

the region by the Romans. Their shaggy coats and hearty resilience developed in response to the harsh climates, after which the cats were then transported to different parts of the world by Norse explorers.

The Norwegian Forest Cat is another ancient breed that carries with it the weight of legends. When Odin disappeared, one legend says, his despondent wife, Freyja, Norse goddess of love and of those slain in battle, rode about searching for him in a golden chariot pulled by large, longhaired cats. Existence of these cats was recorded in the Eddic poems, circa A.D. 800–1200. Known in its native land as the *skogkatt* (translated to mean "forest cat"), the Norwegian Forest Cat was honored by its first cat fancy club in Norway in 1934.

Norwegian Forest Cat

Like the Maine Coon, the "Weegie" is heavily boned, with a powerful, full chest. It has a shorter body, however, with a concentration of muscle in the rear to give it the power to climb the trees in its native forests. This breed is also smaller than the Maine Coon, with its standard calling for a medium size. The coat is double and smooth, with a woolly undercoat for insulation. The Norwegian Forest Cat's coat has a tendency to have long, rather oily, guard hairs that provide further weather-proofing. The winter coat has a magnificent mane to frame the face. Tabby patterns are most common.

The head is triangular and well proportioned in shape, with a straight nose, a firm chin and large, expressive eyes. The ears, decorated with lynx tufts, are medium large, rounded and set more to the side of the head than the top.

Breeders know this breed to be the "strong, silent type," and a natural athlete. It stalks and pounces for the sheer joy of the activity, and is outgoing and friendly to everyone, strangers and family alike.

The Ragdoll

This breed has been around for some years, but its controversial origins have led it to find quicker acceptance by the public than by cat-registering associations. Originally a hybrid breed, it was created by a cross between a white Persian-type female and a seal point Birman male, with offspring later crossed with sable Burmese cats. The controversy stemmed from the breed's originator; this Riverside, California, cabinetmaker claimed that the original female had produced normal kittens until hit by a car in the early 1960s. This accident, according to the breeder, somehow changed the genetic structure of all subsequent kittens. Among the claims she made were that these later kittens were exceptionally large, and had developed an overall serene disposition and a temperament that caused them to go limp in a person's arms (thus the name, Ragdoll). She also claimed that the cats were impervious to pain. With no scientific validation of these claims forthcoming, and after meeting heavy resistance by cat registries, the originator formed her own registry in 1971 and franchised the name.

Ragdoll

Ultimately, people who began seriously breeding these cats split from that independent registry and sought and finally received recognition from the United States

cat associations. The CFA accepted the breed for the Miscellaneous category in 1993, and the breed began its six-year move toward eventual acceptance in championship.

The Ragdoll appears in three patterns: the Colorpoint, the Mitted and the Bi-Color; of these, only the Bi-Color is currently accepted by the CFA. It is a well-balanced cat with no extreme features. Males can tip the scales at up to twenty pounds, while females are proportionately smaller. The body is strongly boned and muscular, and the head is a broad modified wedge with a well-developed chin, a rounded muzzle, and a medium-length nose with a gentle break between the eyes. Eyes are always blue and oval. The coat is plush, silky and medium-long to long.

The Ragdoll is, indeed, docile, mild mannered and congenial. It is playful but not overactive, and has a soft, pleasing voice.

The Turkish Van

Some published sources point to depictions of cats on ornaments recovered from the Mount Ararat region of Turkey from 5000 B.C. to say that this may be the oldest of all the domestic cat breeds. With its cashmere-feeling coat and its unusual (for a cat) love of swimming and water, the Turkish Van is among the most unique of breeds.

As with other breeds, legends abound. One has the ark arriving at Mount Ararat, with Noah trying to keep all the animals aboard from stampeding each other in their eagerness to touch dry land. Two red and white cats simply leaped into the water and swam ashore.

The Turkish Van's affinity for water more likely developed in response to the extreme temperatures in their native region; the Lake Van region of Turkey and the bordering areas of Syria, Iran, Iraq and the old Soviet Union often experience temperatures of above a hundred degrees during the summer. The unique coat has highly efficient water-repelling properties, allowing the cat to take a dip to cool off. It lacks a woolly undercoat and thins in the summer, and with the exception of the plume of its tail, the cat appears almost shorthaired. The winter coat lengthens, and a ruff sometimes develops.

The Vans were introduced to England in 1955, and arrived in the United States in 1983. Like the Turkish Angora, the breed is preserved in its native land; a breeding program exists at the Turkish College of Agriculture in connection with the Ankara Zoo. The Van is a larger, sturdier breed than its more delicate countryman, with a long body, good muscle development and a broad, powerful chest. The muscular hips and pelvis give the cat a swaggering gait. Essentially a white cat, color is confined to the head and tail, with a few random body markings. When a Van has a colored patch between the shoulder blades, it is called the "Mark of Allah" or "thumbprint of God" and is considered good luck in Muslim countries.

Turkish Van

Breeders describe the Turkish Van as energetic, agile and intelligent, and in perpetual motion. Their talkative nature demands attention from their humans, and displays definite imprinting behavior that begets special loyalty to one or two people.

Longhair Variants

For those cat owners who like things "their way," the American registries are trying to be accommodating. In cats, the gene for long hair is recessive to the gene for short hair. This means that cats with only shorthaired ancestors in their pedigrees for many generations can produce longhaired kittens when that elusive, hidden gene is contained in both the sire and the dam.

The gene pools of even the oldest breeds of cat were decimated during World War II Europe, and some bordered on total extinction. When cat fanciers picked themselves up and dusted their hobby off after the rigors of the war, they discovered that some breeds had undergone accidental hybrid matings, and that still others had to be hybridized just to preserve the last remnants of the breed. As a result, even the oldest known shorthaired breeds such as the Siamese might have picked up the recessive factor for long hair. Other, newer breeds that resulted from genetic mutations in free-roaming, free-breeding street or barn cats were harboring this recessive characteristic and therefore introduced it into a proper, human-controlled breeding program.

STATS FOR CATS

Here are tidbits of cat trivia with which you can impress cat lovers (and cats) at cocktail parties and the like. Did you know that . . .

The average weight of an adult male cat is 8.6 pounds, and of an adult female cat, 7.2 pounds.

The largest breed of cat is the Ragdoll. Males weigh 15 to 20 pounds.

The smallest breed of cat is the Singapura, which weighs from 4 to 6 pounds.

The cat has 40 more bones in its body than a human.

The cats Hellcat and Brownie were the sole heirs to the 415,000-acre estate of Dr. William Grier of San Diego when he died in 1963.

(From *The Quintessential Cat*, by Roberta Altman. New York: Macmillan, 1994.)

The end result is that nearly all of the traditionally shorthaired breeds have occasionally produced longhaired kittens, despite the most careful selection to try to eliminate the stubborn gene. Fanciers went through a controversial and confusing period in which certain breeders saw merit in the longhaired variants, while others viewed them as anathemas. Eventually, the registries allowed compromises in which longhair variants were separated from their parent breeds, and then classified as a separate breed. This situation, of course, has provoked still more controversy, and the current movement in the registries is to realign breed definitions yet again to accommodate the longhaired variants.

The CFA has begun the trend toward rejoining breeds and their longharied variants. For example, the longhaired Manx, once separately classified as the Cymric breed, has now been reunited with its parent breed; it is registered and shown as a separate, longhaired division of the Manx. On the other hand, the latest such breed to be registered, the American Curl, was accepted from the beginning with both a longhaired and a shorthaired division. Additionally, other breeds established as shorthaired breeds, such as the Japanese Bobtail and the Scottish Fold, have petitioned for and been granted longhair divisions.

Because of the recent fluctuation regarding classification of longhaired variants, the following discussion could soon be outdated. The associations are currently attempting to create order out of somewhat chaotic breed descriptions, definitions and standards. Each association at this time has its own approach to the situation.

American Curl

The American Curl A natural genetic mutation, the American Curl's outstanding feature is its ears. These ears, set on the corners of the head, have a firm base, yet curve back away from the face in smooth arcs that point toward a central point at the base of the skull. They should, however, not curl so much as to touch the skull. The original mutations were discovered in 1981 in Southern California. Still in its infancy as a breed, the Curl is medium in every way, including size and contours. The coat of the longhaired variety is silky, with minimal undercoat.

The Balinese While the creation of the Himalayan was an attempt to create a Persian with the points of a Siamese, the Balinese is generally accepted to be

the result of a spontaneous longhair mutation of the Siamese that was specifically bred for as early as the 1940s. The Balinese has all the attributes of the Siamese: a long tubular body; svelte, graceful lines; sapphire blue eyes; and a vocal, inquisitive personality. In fact, breeders say that the only difference between the two is the "ermine" coat worn by the Balinese in the traditional seal, blue, chocolate and lilac point colors. The fine coat is of a medium length and lacks a downy undercoat; it therefore lies close to the body, emphasizing the cat's long, slim lines. The tail is plumed.

Balinese

The Longhaired Japanese Bobtail Accepted as a division of the shorthaired version, the Japanese Bobtail is the good-luck cat of Japan. This breed is thought to have been brought to Japan from China or Korea as early as a thousand years ago. It is featured in many ancient prints and paintings, especially in the favored tricolor, Mi-Ke. Japan's isolation as an island allowed this distinctive bobbed-tail breed (both longhaired and shorthaired) to flourish for generations without a significant amount of crossbreeding. Interestingly, the breed began as a spontaneous genetic mutation totally distinct from that which is responsible for the tailless Manx. Each Bobtail's tail has its own unique variation of bends, twists and corkscrews, but they all ideally have a pom-pom–like appearance. This medium-size cat has distinctly Oriental high cheekbones and oval

Longhaired Japanese Bobtail

eyes, and long, slender legs. Very vigorous, healthy and active cats, the Bobtails have an affinity for riding on their human's shoulders and for carrying things in their mouths. They sometimes appear in solid colors, but the majority have bicolored and tricolored coats.

The Longhaired Oriental/Javanese Aficionados of the long, lean, Siamese-styled cats began introducing an astounding variety of colors and color combinations to create today's Oriental Shorthair. That stubborn longhaired gene kept cropping up, however, so Oriental Shorthair breeders began to perpetuate it; some even introduced the Balinese breed to refine the longhaired Oriental's silk chiffon coat. The color-pointed version of this longhaired cat is known as the Javanese. So, a cat lover who prefers the leggy, elegant Siamese body style, but who also desires a full palette of every available cat color and a flowing, silky coat, should find that the Longhaired Oriental is custom-made for him or her. According to breeders, this totally people-oriented cat actively supervises and participates in every household chore, often doing so by giving very vocal instructions. The Longhaired Oriental will find an available lap perfect for naps, and does not discriminate among family or guests, children or adults. Little grooming is required to keep this breed's trouble-free coat in shape.

Longhaired Oriental/ Javanese

The Longhaired Manx (Cymric) Even after trying for over a hundred years, fanciers have been unsuccessful in eliminating the recessive gene for long hair that was probably a part of the breed's earliest heritage. This stubborn gene finally caused breeders and cat associations to create a separate breed for the

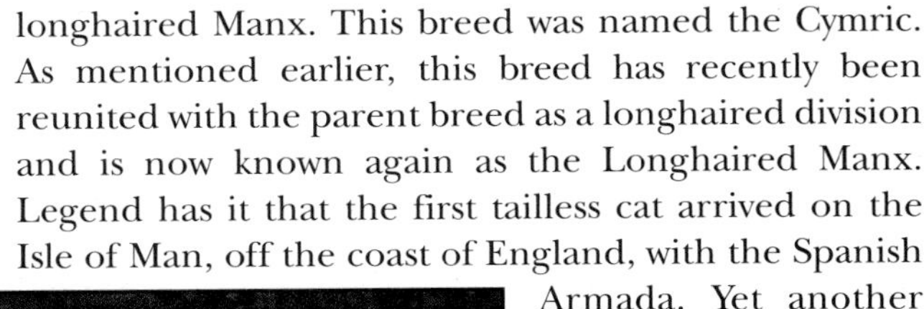

longhaired Manx. This breed was named the Cymric. As mentioned earlier, this breed has recently been reunited with the parent breed as a longhaired division and is now known again as the Longhaired Manx. Legend has it that the first tailless cat arrived on the Isle of Man, off the coast of England, with the Spanish Armada. Yet another fable tells that Noah, in his hurry to secure the Ark to set sail, closed the door on the tails of his last arrivals, the cats; he thus rendered them tailless. There is wide variation in tail length of both the longhaired and the shorthaired Manx; some are born with full tails; some with short tails (called a stumpy); some have a rise of only one vertebra; and yet others (the rumpies) are completely tailless. Only the latter two can be shown in championship competition. The long, yet thick, coat of the variant accentuates its rounded appearance. The Manx is short-bodied and is higher in the hind quarters than in the front. It is solidly muscled, compact and well balanced, and is a powerful jumper. The Manx has been called the clown of the cat world; its breeders insist that it has quite a sense of humor and loves playing practical jokes on its humans. It gets along well with other pets and is known for forming strong human bonds.

Longhaired Manx (Cymric)

The Longhaired Scottish Fold A much more recent import from the British Isles, the Scottish Fold is the result of a natural mutation discovered in a barn cat in Scotland in 1961. Virtually all Scottish Folds descend from that original mutation, a white cat named Susie, whose ears folded forward and downward on her head. This ear gives the breed its unique appearance, which is said to resemble a pixie or a teddy bear or, more fequently, an owl. This cat's face is guaranteed to capture the hearts of cat lovers. In an attempt to increase its gene pool, the Scottish Fold has been crossbred with Persians, Exotics, American Shorthairs and British Shorthairs. The gene that creates the folded ear is a dominant gene with incomplete penetrance, meaning that some kittens will have folded ears and others will have normal ears. All kittens are born with apparently normal ears; signs of folding become evident at approximately three to four weeks of age, when some kittens' ears begin tipping forward and down. Despite attempts by many to limit the breed to shorthairs, some breeders were enchanted by the longhaired version. Never accepted as a breed on its own as was the longhaired Manx/Cymric, the longhaired Scottish Fold was accepted in CFA as a division of the original breed. Like their barnyard ancestors, Scottish Folds are hardy cats with placid dispositions. These seldom-vocal cats are not known to be lap cats; they prefer sitting near their humans to sitting on them.

Longhaired Scottish Fold

Interesting New Breeds

The Siberian Cat It was in England that a "Russian Cat" first appeared in a cat show. Russian cats were also commonly interbred with Persians and Turkish Angoras in the early days of the organized cat fancy to produce what eventually became known as the modern Persian. As a breed, the Siberian cat disappeared from Europe and the United States for many years. Behind the Iron Curtain, though, the breed was perpetuated in the

Siberian Cat

Russian cat registry, a few representatives of which were first imported to the United States in 1990. Descended from the same Northern European ancestors as the Maine Coon and the Norwegian Forest Cat, the Siberian Cat also shares many similar features, including a shaggy, dense coat. The Siberian, however, is more rounded in appearance than the other two breeds, and is quite large. Breeders say that the breed in Russia has produced examples that weigh up to forty-five pounds, but U.S. versions are significantly lighter: Males average sixteen to twenty-six pounds, and females average thirteen to seventeen pounds.

The Selkirk Rex Genes that produce the curly coat found in two shorthaired breeds, the Cornish Rex and the Devon Rex, were natural mutations. It could therefore only be a matter of time before this mutation occurred in a longer-coated cat as well. Voilà! In 1987 the Selkirk Rex was discovered at an animal shelter near the Selkirk Mountains in Wyoming. (The name "Rex" was adopted in all three breeds because of their coats' resemblance to the curly fur of the Rex rabbit.) Still very much in the developmental stage, the original Selkirk Rex was bred to a Persian male, but its progeny has since been mated to British Shorthairs, Persians and Exotics to extend the gene pool. There are both longhaired and shorthaired variants of this medium-size, heavily boned cat, and the Selkirks are accepted in all colors, including pointed. The unique coat is thick and plush and falls in soft, loose curls.

Selkirk Rex

chapter 3

Choosing the Longhaired Cat for You

Choosing a pet is a family decision that should not be undertaken lightly. The pet you choose will become a member of the family for as many as fifteen to twenty years. He or she will require love, attention, care, quality food, training, veterinary checkups, treatment when ill and a whole multitude of other needs—much like any other family member. A whim or spur-of-the-moment decision to adopt or to buy a pet because it's cuddly and cute is the recipe for unhappiness.

What a Cat Has to Offer

Increasing numbers of both families and single people are choosing to add cats to their households. Cats are small, relatively quiet, able to adapt to life in even the smallest apartment and don't require trips outdoors to relieve themselves. The cat can be a comforting, loving

presence without being demanding. The old stereotype that cats are "feminine" animals that should be kept by women, and that dogs, who are innately more masculine, should be left to the men, has long ago been debunked. Men and boys can also enjoy the ease and convenience of owning a cat, as well as appreciate this animal's reserved companionship. Choosing between a cat and a dog should be purely a matter of taste or preference, and not of social convention. More and more families are opting to have both! These two species, while natural enemies in the wild, often join each other as equal members of their human families, bonding in ways that go far beyond simple coexistence. Stories abound of close, loving relationships between cats and dogs.

Cats and dogs can not only live peaceably, they can become the best of friends.

Longhaired or Shorthaired?

After choosing to obtain a cat, all those involved in the decision must then narrow that choice even further. There are more than forty different breeds of cats recognized by the various cat-registering associations, not to mention the even wider array of sizes, shapes and colors of cats available at the local animal shelter; the random-bred, or "Heinz 57," cat is as popular as ever. The most important consideration in choosing a cat, however, should probably be whether to get a longhaired or shorthaired cat.

A longhaired cat can belong to one of the many breeds described in Chapter 2, and there are random-bred cats that have long, plush coats as well. Temperaments and activity levels vary widely, so again the matter of personal preference is paramount. A long-haired cat will need more attention to grooming than a shorthaired cat, but less than most people think!

Shedding First, understand that all cats shed, and longhairs as a general rule will shed more than shorthairs. However, a little-known fact is that the hair shed by a longhaired cat is actually easier to remove from furniture and clothing because of its tendency to clump together; short hairs tend to stick into the fibers. Furthermore, because a well-groomed longhaired cat receives regular combing to remove dead hairs, there is less hair left to fall out and cling to household fabrics.

High-maintenance grooming Again, all cats will benefit from regular grooming and an occasional bath. But even an occasional bath and the five minutes each day with a comb that are necessary to keep the longhair's coat looking clean and tangle-free should not be a hardship for most owners. If you're willing to make this commitment, you'll save both yourself and your cat a lot more hardship in the long run.

There is, however, an additional consideration regarding the kind of coat a particular cat has. The coat of a "single"-coated cat (one without an undercoat) can be either very short, or semi-long and silky. "Double"-coated cats have a dense undercoat in addition to longer guard hairs, which can also range from short and plush to extremely

BLACK CATS

Throughout time, black cats have been both praised as being bearers of great luck and persecuted as harbingers of grave misfortune. The word *felis* is Roman for a good and auspicious omen, though the Romans also called cats *gatta*, meaning weasel.

In the Middle Ages, black cats were associated with sorcery, and many were killed in symbolic ceremonies.

Black cats are linked to fate in many countries. In America it's said that if a black cat crosses your path it's bad luck; in Ireland it foretells death in an epidemic; yet in England and Asia, it means you will have great luck.

Black cats were kept by sailors' wives to ensure their husbands' safety, and have starred in stories and poems by Edgar Allan Poe and William Butler Yeats. More recently, they have been pets to such celebrities as Jimmy Connors and Donna Mills.

long. The denser, double coats tend to mat and shed worse than single coats, and therefore require more diligent care. Keep the presence, or lack thereof, of an undercoat in mind when choosing your cat.

Allergies Most people who claim to be allergic to cats are not actually allergic to cat hair, but rather to the dander produced by the skin. For allergic owners, a longhaired cat, kept properly groomed and bathed to minimize the dander, will often be preferable to a shorthaired cat less scrupulously kept.

A longhaired cat requires more grooming than its shorthaired counterparts.

In summation, a person or family not willing to devote a few minutes a day to combing their cat, or a few hours each month to an occasional bath (or trip to the cat grooming shop), probably shouldn't choose a longhaired cat. If, however, the appeal of a beautiful, long, flowing coat is sufficient reason to make the commitment to grooming a longhaired cat, then we move to further considerations.

Random-Bred or Pedigreed?

Once you've decided to get a longhaired cat, you should then give some thought to whether or not that cat should be random-bred or pedigreed. The same qualities that endear us to the "one hundred percent American mutt" are equally charming in the random-bred cat, and local shelters will have an impressive array of colors and personalities from which to choose. Shelter adoption fees are reasonable, and often include the price of vaccinations and sterilization surgery.

The existence of three-quarter million cats in need of homes should be reason enough for anyone considering obtaining a cat—be it mixed breed or pedigreed—to also consider the merits of adopting a shelter cat. Make the decision that is right for you, but remember that it is possible to get a wonderful and loving pet from one of these organizations.

Purchasing a pedigreed cat, on the other hand, can be particularly advantageous, since the cat's temperament and general "breed attributes" will be relatively more predictable than those of a cat whose background is indefinite. Choosing a breed can be a difficult decision, however. You may find that printed material available for no charge from cat shows and registries can help you further research the breeds that appeal to you.

If you think that a pedigreed cat is out of your price range, check with your local cat club. Many clubs now have purebred rescue programs, and cooperate with local shelters to take responsibility for any abandoned purebred cats. These clubs have the cats fully vetted, vaccinated, neutered or spayed and make them available for a minimal adoption fee. Some of the rarer breeds may require placing your name on a waiting list.

SIGNS OF A HEALTHY KITTEN

What should you look for when trying to determine the health of a kitten you're thinking of buying or adopting? The kitten's eyes should be bright, clear and alert. Her ears should be clean and cool to the touch. Her coat should be plush and lively, with no signs of external parasites and no signs of encrusted scabs on the skin. The kitten should be well fleshed out and muscular, without a distended or tight abdomen (a little kitten pooch on the tummy is normal). As you observe the kitten, she should be aware of her surroundings, and respond to moving stimuli, such as a toy, other kittens or you. The kitten should respond to the human touch. While a shy kitten is not necessarily indicative of a bad pet, that shyness should not cause the kitten to panic when picked up.

Pedigreed kittens are available from a variety of sources in a wide range of prices. A good place to start, if just for the knowledge you'll gain about the breed, is

with a responsible breeder who exhibits his or her cats in sanctioned cat shows. These exhibitors have intimate knowledge of their chosen breed, and can teach a new owner all of the intricacies of proper care and grooming. Purchasers can also schedule an appointment to visit the breeder. It is important to see the breed, and your chosen cat in particular, in its home surroundings. Ask to see the sire and dam of the kitten, and look around with an observant eye to determine whether the kitten has been raised in a clean and loving environment.

Choosing to get a cat from a shelter can give you the chance both to find a wonderful pet and to save a life.

Responsible breeders can be located by contacting the local cat club, your veterinarian, or one of the national cat registeries listed in Chapter 12. It may be that your chosen breed is not available in your local area, and preliminary contact will have to be made by letter or long-distance telephone call. While buying a kitten "sight unseen" and having her shipped in is a fairly common practice, doing so increases the risk of possible mishaps and misunderstandings. If at all possible, plan a visit to the breeder's home to choose your new kitten and to personally escort her home.

Purchasing the Cat

Normal kitten sale contracts contain a health-guarantee provision that will allow the new owner to have the kitten checked by his or her own veterinarian within a reasonable period of time (normally three to seven days) after purchase and to be provided with a full refund if any signs of infectious or contagious illness or congenital or hereditary defects are found.

Most contracts contain additional provisions; take the time to read this contract thoroughly. If there are any provisions that you don't agree with, such as a stipulation that the kitten not be declawed, discuss these issues before signing.

Pet-quality kittens, those that fail to meet the exacting standards required of a show- or breeding-quality cat, usually in some minor way, are sold with a contractual stipulation that the kitten be neutered or spayed at the appropriate age. Often the contract will state that registration papers will be given to the new owner upon proof from a veterinarian that the kitten has been neutered or spayed.

It's hard not to find almost any kitten unbearably cute.

Expect to be interviewed, as well. Responsible breeders like to feel confident that their kittens are going to good homes and that they will be well loved and cared for. You will probably be asked, among other things, about any cats that you may have previously owned, what you know about cat care and about your attitudes regarding declawing and allowing a cat outdoors.

Your new cat should look and feel healthy, happy and full of life.

Pet shops are yet another source of pedigreed kittens. Take the same precautions when purchasing a cat

from a pet shop as you would when purchasing a cat from a breeder. Make sure to carefully inspect the health guarantee. Ask the pet shop for the name, address and telephone number of the breeder from whom the pet shop obtained the kitten you want to purchase. If that person lives nearby, it would be prudent to take the time to visit him or her and observe the conditions in which the kitten was raised. If the breeder lives far away, you might want to ask for the name of that breeder's veterinarian, so that you can ask about the health of his or her cats.

When looking for a kitten, run—don't walk—from:

- Anyone whose written contract does not offer full money back on your kitten if your veterinarian does not certify that she is healthy.
- Anyone whose establishment is dirty or flea-infested.
- Anyone who tries a "hard sell," and is obviously more interested in your money than in the welfare of the kitten.
- Anyone whose cats are not clean or show signs of upper respiratory or skin problems.

Adding a cat to your family is an investment that will be repaid with years of love and companionship.

Before you choose your pet, spend time observing the kittens at play. They should be alert and active and accustomed to interaction with people. Some kittens are naturally more shy than others around strangers, but this shyness should not translate into fear of human touch.

Most importantly, under no circumstances should you purchase a sickly kitten just because you feel sorry for her. As sad as this refusal might be, doing otherwise will merely mean setting yourself up for more heartbreak in the future. The kitten should have been given at least the first series of vaccinations for common viral diseases before she goes to her new home. Many breeders will not place a kitten until she has completed that series, usually at twelve to fourteen weeks of age.

chapter 4

Your Individual Cat

Your cat is like no other cat in the world. His personality has been influenced by genetics, by early kitten experiences, by his bonding and interaction with people, and by the basic independent, curious, loving nature that makes him a cat. Even within lineages, each cat's personality is distinctive. Certain generalities can be drawn, as they have been in Chapter 2, but for every rule there are many exceptions.

In addition to differences in hair length, cats have different kinds of body styles, styles that are often a clue to a cat's underlying temperament. Some cats are obviously built for speed and activity; others are obviously the "couch potato" sort.

As mentioned before, the gene responsible for making a cat have long hair is recessive. Practically speaking, this means that while your cat's parents might both have short hair, if they both carry that recessive gene, your cat will have long hair. Contrary to common opinion, the tabby and the calico are not breeds; they are, rather, pattern/color types, and can be present in many of the different breeds. Similarly, just because a cat has long or short hair does not necessarily mean that his parentage includes any specific breed of cat.

The vast majority of cats are "random bred." They may display the same colors or patterns present in a particular pedigreed cat, but the only way to know if a cat is descended from any particular breed is to trace his heritage through pedigrees and registrations.

Why Cats Stayed Small

While dogs have been purposefully bred, frequently for function, cat breeds have been valued and bred primarily for form and beauty. That's because the cat has had only two functions in its long history: to be a mouser and to be a companion for people. Because the average cat's original size and shape is perfect for fulfilling these functions, there was little need for human intervention to selectively breed for larger, smaller, faster or more massive examples of the species.

While there are some variances in size, cats are, as a whole, a relatively small species.

The average domestic cat will weigh between six and ten pounds at adulthood, though some breeds will grow to be somewhat larger. The Maine Coon and the Ragdoll are more massive cats than average and can top twenty pounds; the Turkish Angora and the Balinese, on the other hand, tend to be on the more petite side of the spectrum.

Selective Breeding

Only in the mid-1800s did people begin recognizing and perpetuating the distinct breeds solely for their beauty. Mother Nature operated with a relatively free hand over the centuries, but humans soon began exerting their influence. Even so, fewer than ten percent of all cats today are pedigreed cats. The vast majority of these pedigreed cats are kept inside as either neutered or spayed pets, or are maintained within controlled breeding environments; relatively few have contributed to free-breeding feral colonies.

The Origins of Coat Colors

People are always fascinated by the many colors and patterns that can dress a cat's coat, regardless of whether that cat is random-bred or pedigreed, longhaired or shorthaired. The original domestic cat was a shorthaired brown mackerel tabby (sometimes called a gray tabby). This cat's coat has a warm fawn ground color and black vertical stripes, both of which provide camouflage in foliage as the predatory cat stalks its prey. The first mutation probably occurred when the stripes were replaced by whorls and broader bands of black, creating what is now known as the classic tabby.

A cat's coat, while beautiful, is also a highly functional means of protection.

As cats moved into safe barns and warm households, camouflage became unnecessary. The tabby mutated into solid colors, the first of which was probably the solid black cat. Mother Nature then began exercising her artistic bent in earnest. The red cat appeared, again by a genetic mutation, and became set in the genetic code as a sex-linked gene. A red cat mated with a black cat produces a female with tortoiseshell markings where both red and black mingle. As a result of this sex linkage in color, all tortoiseshells and their particolored cousins, the blue creams and calicos, are female. On rare occasions, a male tortie will appear, but he will almost invariably be sterile.

Paler variants of tabbies, reds, blacks and tortoiseshells are the results of yet another gene mutation. Black cats with this "dilution" gene became blue (commonly known as gray), red cats became cream, and tortoiseshells became blue creams.

Still another pattern appeared to reflect the increasing domestication of the cat. The piebald gene, which adds portions of white fur to other colors, is present only in domesticated animals that have no need for camouflage. Any color can combine with the piebald gene to create an incredible array of combinations and patterns. Thus, one litter can contain a kitten with just white toes and a bib of white, one with pinto pony–type splashes of color on a white background, and even a white cat with color confined only to the head and the tail.

The original tabby cat underwent even further mutations. In addition to the striped (mackerel) pattern, the swirled (classic) pattern and the ticked pattern in which each individual hair is banded, the tabby can be found in brown, silver, red, blue, cream and "patched" (tortoiseshell and tabby patterns combined) colors as well. This patched coat arose from the "agouti" gene, mutations of which created the shaded and smoke variants, in which the undercoat is white and the guard hairs are tipped with a color.

All animals have the possibility of an albino mutation. In cats, more than one form of albinism appears. In one form, the genetic color code is "hidden," and what we see is a white cat. Rather than the classic pink eyes of the true albino, however, this "odd-eyed" white cat's eyes can be either copper, blue or one of each. There is a tendency for both blue-eyed and odd-eyed white cats to be deaf.

In the second form of albinism, an unusual genetic activity restricts full expression of color to the cooler parts of the cat's body—the face, tail and feet. The body is a much paler shade, either cream or white. This form of albinism is what gives the pointed cats, most notably the Siamese, Himalayan and Birman, their unique markings.

With the advent of the organized cat fancy in the mid-1800s, people began to create an even more incredible variety of colors and patterns. The Persian alone is described in ninety-seven different colors and color/pattern combinations by the CFA.

THE EYES HAVE IT

A cat's eyes are truly unique. They are large and seated deep within the skull. This limits the amount the eyeball can move, but it allows for excellent peripheral vision, especially of moving objects. That is why the cat will dart its head to the side once it's detected movement from the side.

The vertical pupil responds quickly to changes in light, enlarging in the dark and closing to a slit in bright light. Cats are somewhat nearsighted; they can't see close-up objects too well. The pupils also close to a slit to help cats focus on nearby objects. Cats can see a limited range of colors.

All cat owners know that their kitty's eyes are hypnotic. They're the stuff of myth and legend, and even have a gemstone (cat's-eye) named after them. This stone has been used to protect people from witchcraft, make people invisible, and prevent women from getting pregnant when their husbands were away.

Function as Well as Form

While a cat's fur is certainly his crowning glory, there is more to it than just beauty. A healthy coat of fur is your cat's first layer of protection against the environment. The smooth loose-lying layers of well-groomed fur provide a barrier of insulation. In cold weather, body heat is maintained as the cat grooms himself, his saliva smoothing the hair out into an efficient insulator.

Grooming also comes in handy during the warmer months. Cats have sweat glands, but only on the paws of their feet. Obviously, this means of self-cooling isn't particularly effective, so the cat elevates and "fluffs up" his coat in order to allow air circulation. When particularly hot, cats can pant, but tend to cool themselves more often by licking their fur. The evaporation of the remaining saliva accounts for as much as a third of a cat's evaporative-cooling process.

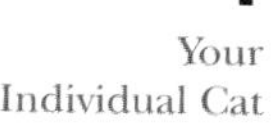

Cats frequently tug at their fur with their teeth when grooming. This seemingly painful practice is actually another way of keeping the coat healthy. Tugging at the hair stimulates the sebaceous glands in the skin to produce sebum. When the cat grooms himself, he spreads the sebum around on his fur, lubricating and waterproofing it. In addition, the cholesterol contained in the sebum is converted by sunlight into Vitamin D, which helps maintain healthy bones and teeth, and aids in the absorption and utilization of calcium and phosphorus. Your cat will absorb much of his nutritional requirement of Vitamin D just by washing himself.

A cat's musculoskeletal structure provides him with extreme flexibility.

The Bones Underneath

As different as a Persian may look from a Turkish Angora, they still share much in common physically. The muscles that hold a cat's skeleton together allow an incredible range of movement. In fact, your cat is so flexible that he can twist his spine one hundred eighty degrees. Part of the reason for this "gumby-like" quality is the number of vertebrae a cat has in his spine—five more than in that of a human. Additionally, the cat's shoulder blades are located on the sides of his body, allowing movement of the front limbs in almost every direction. These shoulder blades are attached to muscle rather than a collarbone, which is why your cat can practically turn his head around backward.

Locomotion

The graceful, fluid stride that most cats possess is due in part to their being digitigrade; they walk on their toes! This characteristic, combined with his unique shoulder blade placement, gives the cat his unique and distinctive gait.

Don't be fooled by the daintiness of your cat's walk, however. An adult cat doesn't waste any time getting where he wants to go; he can run nearly thirty miles an hour when pressed. He uses his tail for balance when rounding corners and when demonstrating typical cat curiosity by exploring precarious heights. Cats love to be up high, and tend to get there by jumping and climbing. Many domestic cats can jump up to five times their own height. The only problem is getting back down; while curved cat claws are ingeniously designed for climbing, they're not so good for descending. Most cats figure out a way to shimmy down backwards, but a few have been caught high up in a tree, reduced to meowing for help from their owners.

Cats are magnificent tree climbers—and not-so-good tree descenders.

Connoisseurs of Touch

As anyone who's spent any amount of time around a cat knows, cats are extremely tactile creatures. They love to be touched, and will go to great lengths to get a pat on the head or a scratch down the spine. A cat's skin is covered with tiny pressure-sensitive lumps, making the whole skin extremely touch-sensitive. Contact with even a single hair on a cat's body will trigger a response in the pressure point nearest that hair, and will alert the cat to a nearby presence.

A cat's whiskers are even more sensitive than the rest of the hair on his body. These vibrissae are set deep into the skin and serve as a kind of antennae. The whiskers help protect your cat's eyes by triggering a blink reflex when something comes into contact with them. They also help your cat judge distance by sensing air pressure and currents in relation to close objects. Many a curious cat has been saved much discomfort by his whiskers; when sticking his head into a small opening, they let him know whether or not the rest of him will fit. In combination with his good night vision, a kitty's whiskers will also help him sense the presence of hidden dangers in darkness.

Super Smellers

While a cat's sensitivity to touch is quite extreme, even more extraordinary is his sense of smell. Smell is one of the most important of the cat's senses, even more important than taste. Newborn kittens use their sense of smell to find their way to their mother, to make claim on a preferred nipple at feeding time and to return time and again the same scent-marked place. Cats mark their territory with scent, express dominance by marking areas with urine and other excretions and in general live their lives with their nose in the lead. Think about all the things they can smell that we can't; while humans have five to twenty million scent analyzing cells, cats have sixty-seven million!

Cats have larger eyes than any other carnivore.

Cats' Eyes

As important as smell is, cats still rely more on their vision to make their way in the world than anything else. As hunters, they use their sharp vision to find their prey, be it a mouse under the kitchen cabinet or a dust bunny under the bed.

A cat's eyes are larger than those of any other carnivore. If your eye-to-face ratio were the same as your cat's, your eyes would be eight inches across! The extreme size of feline eyes, along with their location, gives the cat almost two hundred eighty degrees of three-dimensional sight. Unlike that of a human, a cat's peripheral vision is sharper than his straight-ahead vision, and causes him to be quite nearsighted. It's also much easier for cats to see things in motion than it is for them to see stationary objects.

Many cats use their natural acrobatic ability to show who rules the roost.

Despite these limitations, cats still possess a legendary ability to see in darkness. They need only one-sixth the illumination level humans need in order to see, and make use of twice as much available light. Just as few things are hidden from a cat's eyes in the darkness, neither are those eyes themselves easily hidden in the dark. Light is reflected off the mirrorlike *tapetum lucidum*, a layer of cells in the back part of the cat's eye, and is then reflected back out through the retina to augment vision. This light is what you see when you find a pair of eerie glowing eyes peering at you from the foot of the bed at night.

Super Ears, Too

Ever wonder why it is your cat always seems to jump at even the slightest noise? It's probably because what seems like just a small peep to you is actually quite a big sound to your cat. The radar-dish–like ears of a cat can rotate one hundred eighty degress, funneling sounds down into the ear canal. Especially attuned to high-pitched sounds, cats can hear sounds of up to 60,000 cycles per second. People with even the sharpest ears can hear only about 20,000 cycles per second. Conversely, humans have a much stronger sensitivity to low pitches than do cats. This explains why most cats respond better to people with high-pitched voices.

Tightrope Walkers

If your cat joined the circus, he could most certainly be a brilliant performer on the tightrope. An uncanny sense of balance, good vision, an especially flexible spine and a natural equilibrium provide the cat with everything he needs to perform magically in the air.

When falling, a cat will twist and turn, correcting his position to allow him to almost always land on his feet. There are a few stipulations, however: The cat must be awake, and he must have enough space between his starting position and the ground in which to turn. A fall from a child's arms can endanger your cat by not allowing enough time or distance for him to correct his posture. Similarly, a fall from too great a height can be problematic. Too much time to fall can cause a cat to lose his perfect four-footed landing, and can result in broken legs and even a split jaw.

MYTHS AND SUPERSTITIONS ABOUT CATS

- A cat has nine lives.
- Cats' eyes shine at night because they are casting out the light they gathered during the day.
- When a cat's whiskers droop, rain is coming.
- If you want to keep a cat from straying, put butter on its feet.
- If a cat sneezes near a bride on her wedding day she will have a happy marriage.
- A man who mistreats his cat will die in a storm.
- Stepping over a cat brings bad luck.

An Extraordinary Creature

With all these characteristics taken into account, it seems that there must be only a few creatures that measure up to the extraordinary nature of the cat. It is perhaps this natural excellence in almost everything the cat engages in that has caused it to be both so revered and so feared. Intriguing, aloof, humorous and an endless source of wonder, the cat is sure to continue fascinating humans who endeavor to unravel the mysteries of feline existence.

Living
with Your

part two

Longhaired Cat

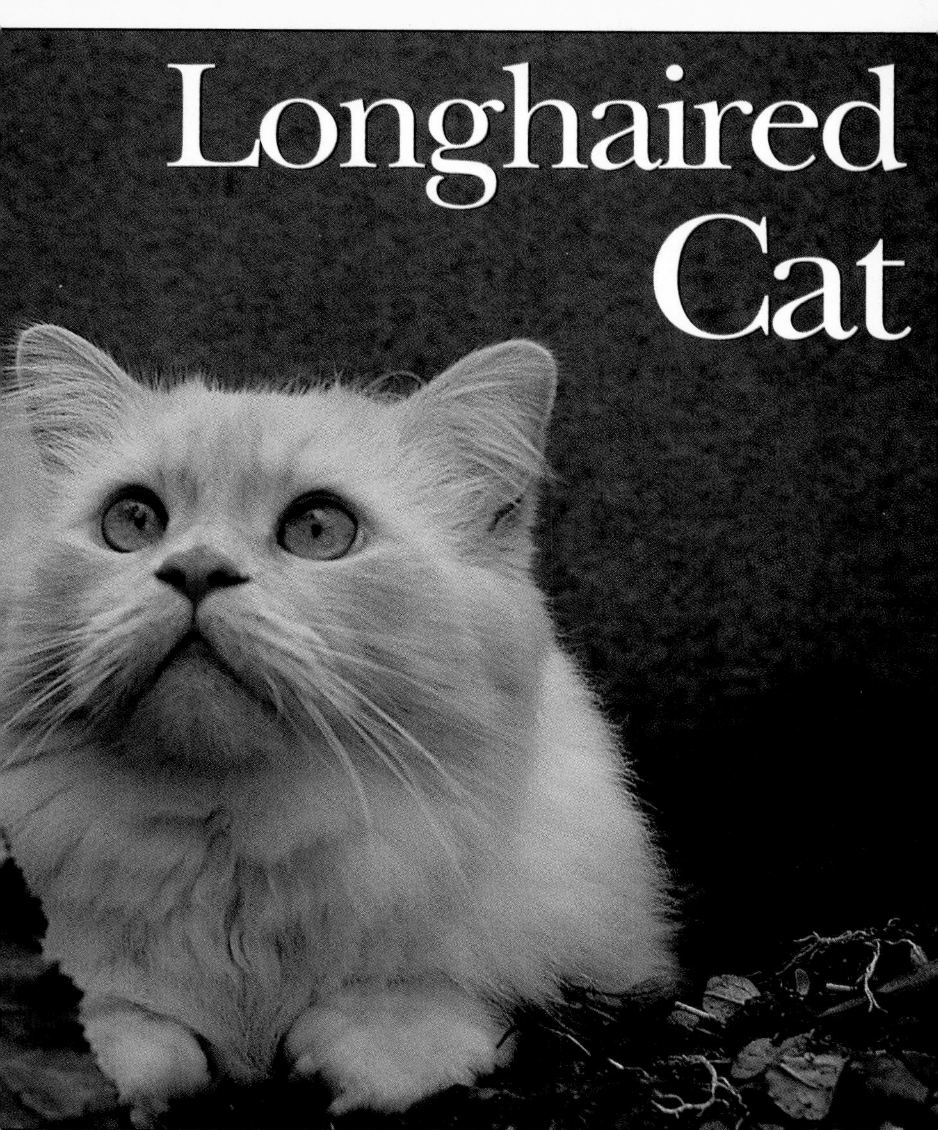

chapter 5

Your Cat and Your Home

You have carefully selected your new kitten, and now it's baby's coming-home day. You should have already arranged to have your kitten's basic needs taken care of. Try to introduce your new kitten on a weekend so that you can be at home with her and help resolve her fears at suddenly being thrust into a totally strange new environment. Among the items that should already be prepared and waiting for the new arrival are:

A litter box and litter Litter boxes come in all sorts of sizes and shapes. Some are covered; some have unique filtration or waste-straining systems; some are colored and some are plain white. Any of them will do the job. A covered litter box hides kitty's waste from human eyes, and helps keep litter from being flung out of the box onto the floor. If the kitten is quite small, she might need a litter box with lower sides to begin with, graduating to boxes with higher sides as she grows.

Litter, of course, is what goes into the litter box. This seemingly simple product, however, is available in a staggering array of choices. There is clumping litter, recyclable litter, litter made from wood shavings or corn husks, scented litter, flushing litter and plain clay litter. The owner of a new longhaired kitten will likely want to avoid the convenient, lightweight materials, because of their tendency to cling to kitty's fur. Otherwise, you'll find litter scattered throughout the house. Scented litter is nice for the human nose, but may offend the kitten; if you have chosen scented litter and find the kitten avoiding it, you will probably want to try one that is unscented. The clumping litter has garnered a large market share because of the ease of maintenance it allows; this comes at a price, however, and even some clumping litters are better than others. The old, standard clay litter is the most economical choice, and has served cats well for many years.

A combination scratching post and cat perch will provide hours of amusement for both you and your cat.

If your kitten is not a "dig to China" sort, you might appreciate the convenience of litter tray liners. These are plastic liners that can be lifted, along with the soiled litter, out of the litter box, tied and disposed of without the need to wash the box. A homemade version can be made from a plastic garbage bag large enough to fit entirely over the litter box. Leave the open end to the side or underneath, so that when you invert it and lift, all of the soiled litter will stay inside the bag.

Even the best litter box and litter will do no good if the kitten can't find them! In Chapter 9, you'll find more on giving your new kitten her own room, or "den," where she will spend her time when you're not at home. The kitten's box should go in this room so that she can become thoroughly familiar with where it is. In very large houses, more than one litter box will be helpful, at least at first. Momcat has introduced the kitten to what litter boxes are used for, so most cats will not have to be trained to use one.

Food and water dishes Just the basics here will do. A baked ceramic or stainless-steel dish will be easiest to thoroughly clean. Feeding wet food on disposable plastic-coated paper plates might be worthwhile as a time-saver.

Some cats find catnip is extremely stimulating; others aren't affected by it.

A scratching post The kitten should not need to go a day without her own scratching post. These are available in a wide range of styles and prices. They should be tall enough that an adult cat can scratch with her full body stretched out and her front legs extended. Many cats seem to prefer scratching posts at a slight angle to ones that are fully upright. Scratching posts that are covered with a material *other* than carpet are best—this way your kitten won't get confused when you encourage her to scratch the carpet on the post, and then reprimand her for scratching the carpet on the floor. Posts covered with tightly wound sisal rope are excellent, but some scratching posts made from real trees, with bark intact, are ideal. Even a log left year round near the hearth can be used by the kitten to maintain her claws. If the kitten is reluctant to use the post that you have provided, try rubbing it with some catnip to make it more appealing. Toys attached to the scratching post

can help make it more attractive to even the most doubtful cat.

A collar and ID tag Generally, collars and long-haired cats, particularly Persians, do not mix. Even well-fitting collars tend to chafe and cause unattractive hair loss. Your kitten, however, should have some means of identification in case she ever gets outside and becomes lost. If the kitten is microchipped, it will make the collar and ID tag unnecessary. There will be further discussion of this subject later in this chapter.

While there may be some "old guard" opposition to a young upstart, the social nature of most cats will shortly smooth things out.

Toys A kitten's favorite toy requires no batteries, but does have many moving parts and is a limitless source of amusement. That toy is you. A kitten can also find untold fun in empty paper sacks or boxes, wadded paper or aluminum foil, a plastic medicine container into which a couple of dry beans have been placed to provide a rattle, or any number of other free items. If you do decide to purchase kitten toys, though, avoid any objects with small parts that can be chewed off and ingested by the kitten. Small bells are a particular danger to cats. Another means of entertainment for your cat might be catnip. While some cats seem not to be greatly affected by this natural herb, most respond pleasurably to its nerve-stimulating properties.

A carrier Sturdy, molded-plastic carriers are available at a reasonable cost from almost any store that carries pet supplies, as well as from pet shops, cat shows and airline cargo departments. This carrier will be well worth the minimal investment by providing both physical and emotional security for your kitten. This will begin with her original trip to your home and will include visits to the veterinarian, the groomer and any traveling you do with your cat. Carriers are available in a variety of sizes.

"Oops" supplies Kittens are babies, and babies do have accidents, as well as some stomach upsets. It would be helpful to have cleaning supplies on hand to make sure that all scent is removed from the site of the accident, not only for the sake of your furniture and carpet, but also to ensure that the kitten is not tempted by the scent to repeat the accident. Most problems can be handled by removing any solid matter carefully with a paper towel, and then saturating the area with a specially designed product for removing scent. Enzyme carpet spot cleaners are the most thorough kind, and can be purchased at most major pet-supply retailers. In a pinch, saturating the spot with a vinegar solution, or working baking soda into the moisture-soaked area, will do the job. If the kitten shows any interest in going back to that spot, discourage this behavior by covering the spot with a tied-off knee-high ladies' stocking filled with either mothballs or lemon peel. Both of these are odors the kitten will find offensive and will want to avoid.

KITTY'S BASIC NEEDS

These are the things all kittens need, and you're better off getting them *before* your kitten comes home, so you're prepared.

food dish

water dish

cat carrier

collar

identification tag

grooming tools

litter tray

bed

first aid kit

harness and leash

Once you have these few cat necessities, as well as the grooming tools discussed in Chapter 7, you have the basics for introducing a kitten to your home. The single most purchased and unused item for kittens is a bed. Buy one if you feel you must, but expect the kitten to choose her own bed, and most likely it will be yours. For her time of confinement during training, a small box or plastic dishpan lined with a towel or rug will give the kitten a cozy napping bed. Longhaired cats actually prefer to sleep on cooler surfaces, especially during warm weather. Their full-length fur coat causes them to seek out marble, tile or wood as a preferred sleeping place, though nippy winter weather can send them scurrying to bed with you for a night's snuggle.

A New Cat and Your Other Pets

If you already have a pet at home, an introductory period for him and the new cat will be necessary. While pet psychology books laud the "let them sniff through a door first" method, the pets will likely learn to accommodate one another's presence quite easily on their own. Care should be taken, however, to prevent one of the pets being harmed by the other. A rambunctious dog might need to be restrained as the kitten explores, and certainly should be watched for a time to make sure no aggression against the newcomer is likely. Many are the times that a back-arched, two-pound kitten has faced down a dog, even one as big as a Great Dane. Be aware that some breeds of dog specifically bred for chasing or killing "varmints" can be especially aggressive. If your dog is of this sort, keep an eye on him until you're quite convinced that the dog understands that the new kitten is a member of the family, not prey or an unwanted trespasser.

A shy newcomer will quickly feel quite comfortable in his new home.

An older cat, when faced with a newcomer, will usually feel obligated to tell the young upstart that it is decidedly unwanted, and ugly as well! This attitude is understandable, but the cat's inherent curiosity is sure to overcome her original pangs of jealousy. Be sure that claws are clipped on both the older cat and the new kitten so that no damage can be done; one might feel obligated to give the other a cursory smack for emphasis. A few, usually very few, older cats will simply not accept a new companion, especially a young one. The older cat may respond with a period of pouting that gives way to a practice of simply ignoring the newcomer, and eventually turns into a display of veiled interest from a distance. Ordinarily the two will eventually become at least tolerant of one another, and most likely friends. The time frame for this will vary

depending on the individual cats' personalities. In the meantime, though, be sure to give your dog or cat at home special attention while they adjust to their new housemate.

Kitten-Proofing Your Home

Kitten-proofing your home should be done before the newcomer's arrival. Doing so primarily involves removing items of danger to the kitten, and putting up certain cherished breakable items until the kitten has learned her house manners. Walk through your home on the lookout for anything harmful that the kitten could ingest or in which she could become entangled. Twist ties for bread wrappers, for instance, are both an appealing toy for a kitten and a terrible danger if swallowed. Pincushions or sewing needles should be put out of harm's way. Caustic or toxic chemicals should not be left out, and any insect traps or poison bait should be removed.

> **WHAT EVIL LURKS . . .**
>
> Before your kitten gets too used to living the indoor/outdoor life, consider the dangers to which she'll be exposed in the "natural" world:
>
> cars and other traffic
>
> parasites (ticks, fleas, worms)
>
> other cats
>
> dogs
>
> wildlife (including rabid animals)
>
> toxic chemicals
>
> unsympathetic neighbors
>
> This doesn't mean your kitten can never go outside. You can build or buy a variety of enclosures or teach your kitten to walk in a harness on leash, then the two of you can explore together.

Remember that the kitten is not strictly horizontal, so as you scan for these potential hazards, look above floor level as well. Electrical cords, if possible, should be kept out of the kitten's reach; chewing on them can cause terrible burns on the mouth and even death. An alternative, especially with a teething kitten, is to purchase plastic tubes from an automobile supply shop to cover exposed electrical cords. Plastic plug-in socket guards, available from hardware stores, can also prevent possible electrocution.

Cats have an unfortunate propensity for drinking from toilet bowls; more than one kitten has fallen in. Automatic-release toilet bowl disinfectants are hazardous should your kitten drink them, so toilet lids should be kept down.

Many common house plants are toxic to cats, and can cause anything from mild gastric upset to death. These plants are listed in Chapter 8. It is still possible to maintain living foliage in your home; just avoid those that can cause your kitten or cat harm.

Another hazard for kittens or cats, who seek dark, warm spots for naps, is the clothes dryer, and in some cases the clothes washer as well. Make sure that your kitten has not slipped past you and burrowed under the clothes before these appliances are turned on. Kittens have also been known to investigate the inside of refrigerators, and a quick scan before closing the door will insure the kitten's safety.

Give your cat something safe to play with, such as a ball of yarn; this will help keep her out of mischief.

Christmas may be the single most hazardous time for cats and kittens. Not only are virtually all of the traditional Christmas plants (holly, mistletoe, etc.) toxic, but the glittering array of shiny ornaments dangling from the tree (and after all, trees *are* meant for climbing) are more than a self-respecting kitten can allow to go uninspected. For the kitten's safety, replace the breakable ornaments with others made of paper, fabric, metal or wood, at least at the base of the Christmas tree. The tree itself should be secured so that it cannot be tipped over by a climbing kitten. Christmas trees can be lovely without the use of the deadly angel's hair (which is spun glass), and by

replacing easily ingested tinsel strips with colorful garlands or popcorn strings.

The kitten's room for confinement during training should be even more kitten-proofed, and should contain nothing that can harm the kitten, or that the kitten can damage or break. You might want to purchase a specially designed cat cage, therefore eliminating the need for a separate room. A bathroom or a laundry room can also serve the purpose, however. A single bedroom is yet another option, assuming that the kitten cannot get into any mischief in that room, and that it provides nothing to confuse the kitten about what is and what is not allowed in her household manners.

DOG-PROOFING KITTY'S DOMAIN

Do you already have a dog? Even the best-trained pooch is tempted to sample cat food—or worse, clean up Kitty's aromatic bathroom deposits. To solve the problem, place Kitty's food and litter box where the dog can't reach them. For adult cats, elevating litter boxes and food bowls can be the answer, but tiny kittens less able to jump and climb need other options.

A covered litter box with an opening Kitty enters from below foils most dogs. Consider using two: one for Kitty's bathroom and the other to protect her food. Don't worry; Kitty will know which is which.

Try folding accordion-style baby gates to close off doorways or portions of rooms from Poochie. Choose one with lattice openings large enough for Kitty to go through, or cut a kitten-size opening too small for a dog.

Or, protect Kitty's domain with upside-down plastic milk crates placed over bowls and litter pans. Cutting a kitten-size opening lets her come and go but keeps snoopy Poochie out of her hair.

Hopefully, by this time you will have made the conscientious choice not to allow your kitten outdoors to face the hazards of disease, larger animals, parasites and automobiles, to name just a few. It is sheer fallacy that a cat must be outdoors to be happy. A cat can enjoy the sunshine, birds and butterflies from the safety of a window. By all means, if your home's windows are not easily accessible to the kitten, provide her with a window ledge (available at larger pet-supply stores) and, until the kitten grows large enough to make the jump, a means of getting to it, such as a stool. Open balconies, however, present the danger of the kitten either falling, or overestimating her leaping ability, both of which can result in broken bones. Even screened windows and doors should be secured so they cannot be pushed out. The indoors environment can be just as stimulating and enjoyable to the cat with very little effort on your part, and its safety cannot be overrated.

Cat owners can even provide for the cat's natural tendency to eat grass. Cats and other animals instinctively seek out grass to eat, and indoor cats often resort to house plants, which, even if not toxic, can be shredded into an unattractive mess. Eating grass is beneficial, since it contains a higher concentration of chlorophyl, enzymes, antioxidants, vitamins, minerals and amino acids than almost any other food, and wheat grass has the highest concentration of these nutrients of all grass types.

A pot of home-grown wheat grass can provide the indoor cat with a taste of the great outdoors.

Allowing Your Cat Outdoors

Among the perils a cat will face outside are viral and bacterial diseases; fleas, ticks and other parasitic insects; poisonous lawn chemicals; cars; dogs or wild animals that view your cat as prey; other cats that can inflict painful wounds that can become infected; and the very real danger that she could be lost—perhaps chased out of the neighborhood by a pursuing dog. A few minutes of rolling in the grass is not worth the risk. If you choose to take the risk, common sense will have surely dictated that any cat that is to go outside will not be declawed; declawing eliminates the cat's ability to climb or to protect herself from dangers.

There is also the ever-present danger that an outdoor cat will be picked up or trapped by animal control. Even if your cat is kept safely inside, there remains the possibility that a door will be left ajar, allowing your cat to venture outside. For your cat's safety, whether she's allowed to go outside or is kept indoors, do consider having her permanently identified with a microchip.

In the early years of microchipping, there was a problem with standardization—one manufacturer's scanner would not detect the presence of another manufacturer's chip. The technology for microchipping has finally been refined and standardized; the chip is now commonly used, and is very safe for the animal.

The chip, which is only a little larger than a grain of rice, is inserted by your veterinarian under the skin in the cat's shoulder in much the same way that a vaccine is administered. A few minutes of inactivity allows the chip to "set" in place. Shelters now commonly check each incoming animal with a scanner to detect the presence of a microchip ID. Several manufacturers offer reasonably priced programs by which the owner's name, address and phone number are recorded in a database along with the pet's individual ID number. Ordinarily, this involves a one-time fee to both insert the chip and record the information. The owner must, of course, remember to notify the registering organization in case of a change of address.

When a shelter scans the cat and finds the number, it is then a simple matter to trace the owner so the cat can be safely returned. Owner reluctance to put collars

GROWING WHEAT GRASS FOR YOUR CAT

You can grow wheat grass for your cat at home by purchasing organic hard wheat berries (about 1 tablespoon for each crop) from most health food stores. Soak the wheat berries overnight in water. Drain off the water and allow the wheat berries to air dry on a piece of paper towel.

Scatter the berries over approximately 1 inch of potting soil in a ceramic bowl, and spray with water. (Health food experts say that adding kelp to the water will achieve a hardier crop of grass.) Cover the single layer of wheat berries with 1/4 inch of peat moss or soil. Keep the soil moist, but avoid overwatering, as this will cause mold.

Place in a bright area. Grass should be ready for your cat in about ten days.

and tags on their cats (out of fear that the collar will hang up on a fence and thus choke the cat) is probably the single most prevalent reason that pet cats face euthanasia in shelters. Microchipping can literally mean the difference between life and death for your cat, whether she is allowed outside on a regular basis, or whether that one accident occurs, and the indoor cat gets out and becomes lost.

Though it remains a controversial issue, some cities or counties require that cats, like dogs, be licensed. Proof of rabies vaccination is required for this licensing, and it is renewed annually. To determine whether this requirement exists in your city or county, telephone your animal control office or your veterinarian and inquire.

Other cities and counties have in place confinement ordinances, or "leash laws," for cats as well as dogs. Practically speaking, this means that you do not have the option to allow your cat out of doors; cats are rarely confined by fences, or by leashes. If your cat is picked up by animal control and found in violation of either licensing or confinement ordinances, you will be subject to fines as well as reclaim penalties and fees.

Other local ordinances that may affect the ownership of your cat include limits on the number of pets that can be owned; nuisance ordinances; and health and sanitation ordinances. While your neighbor may be a thoroughly unreasonable cat hater, he or she is quite legitimately granted by cities the right to enjoy his or her private property free of incursion or nuisance that may be caused by your cat.

It is a simple fact that the cat that is kept indoors is a happier, healthier cat with a life expectancy far beyond those allowed to go outside.

chapter 6

Feeding Your Cat

The cat is an obligate carnivore. What this means is that his body properly assimilates only the protein found in meat. Million-dollar research facilities contribute to the ever-growing body of knowledge about the cat's other nutritional needs, and as much attention is paid to how tasty the finicky feline's next meal will be as to what trace minerals will keep him in prime condition.

Veterinarians attest that pet food is truly a "you get what you pay for" product, so the average consumer has an easy measuring stick for just how well fed his or her cat will be. Recent proliferation of the so-called "premium" cat foods has caused them to line the shelves of major pet retail stores and veterinarians' offices, joining the more commercial "grocery store" variety. Specially formulated foods for all stages of the cat's life, and for special health needs, are available as well.

What Kind and How Often

As a general rule, seek out only those foods whose labels state that they are "complete and balanced" as established by the Association of American Feed Control Officials (AAFCO). Ingredients listed on pet food labels are often difficult for the average consumer to recognize, so this kind of identification can be reassuring. How well your cat utilizes the particular food can be gauged by observing his stool. Poor-quality protein cannot be assimilated, and will result in loose or diarrheal stools. If the stool is excessive, too much fiber or filler was used in that brand of food. If either of these is a problem, consider moving up to a premium food. When you first get your kitten, continue using the brand that he has become accustomed to. If you do decide that you would like to change brands, do so gradually.

Generally speaking, a kitten should be fed special kitten formulations until it is six to eight months old. These foods contain added calcium needed for growing bones and teeth, as well as added calories needed for active kittens. Adult, or maintenance, foods will do nicely for most cats. Less-active indoor cats may need a formula that contains reduced calories to avoid the dangers of obesity, especially as they age.

GOOD AND BAD SNACKS

Besides feeding a high-quality commercial cat food, you can feed your cat some people foods—occasionally, and always as part of the cat's regular diet. Always consider total caloric intake and if you're going to treat Kitty, reduce his regular meal somewhat. Be careful what you give as treats. Here are some good ones (+) and bad ones (-):

+ vegetables, raw or cooked, without sauce

+ broth from water-packed meats and fish

+ cooked meat (poultry, beef, lamb, pork, liver), with any and all bones removed

+ cheese or yogurt

+ fresh fruit

- raw fish

- uncooked meats

- dog food

- bones of any kind

- chocolate in any form

- candies, desserts, sweets

- onions and raw potatoes

Types of Food

Cat foods come in dry, moist and semimoist states. As a general rule, the semimoist foods contain excess additives and dyes that are unhealthful for your cat. A combination of dry and moist (canned) foods is preferred.

Kittens should be offered at least two meals of canned food daily. As a rule of thumb, the amount of food offered should be what the kitten will eat in an hour. If you return to the plate after that hour has elapsed and find food still there, remove the leftovers, and at the next meal offer less. If you find that the kitten has polished off the entire plate, at the next meal offer more. In either event, pick up the plate after an hour.

A kitten has different nutritional needs than an adult cat.

This method of feeding will prevent a kitten from developing the "finicky" habits for which cats are known. If wet food is left out all day, it loses its palatability and will spoil. Additionally, when food is available at all times, the cat will quickly become bored with it. By limiting the time for which it is offered, the cat will learn that if he does not eat the food when it's made available, it will not be there later. Each meal, then, becomes a treat.

Dry food can be left out at all times, but should be changed at least every other day, since it tends to go stale. It is particularly important that cats who eat primarily dry food have fresh water available at all times. Most dry food will contain less than ten percent water; canned food contains seventy percent or more water, so the cat will drink less if fed primarily canned food.

Adult cats can continue on the twice-daily wet food feedings, or can receive it only once, with dry food supplementing those feedings. The cat's tendency to obesity should be a guide in this choice. If the cat begins to put on excess weight, it may be necessary to offer dry food in controlled amounts once or twice a day, rather than leaving it out for free feeding.

Special Considerations

Just as with people, perhaps the most important health consideration for cats is a good diet in combination with exercise, which will help avoid the stress that excess poundage puts on all body organs, especially the heart. A frequently fatal condition known as feline hepatic lipidosis is also known to strike obese cats. If your cat's gastronomic delights lead him to overeat, then the special "light" diets for less active cats may be necessary. Cats tend to become "couch potatoes," and should be offered interesting new toys to encourage activity. Owners can participate in games that stimulate activity. A wadded aluminum foil ball or some feathers tied to the end of a string attached to a piece of dowel rod can keep you in your easy chair even while you play "go fish" with the cat.

A cat allowed to eat too many flavorful treats may become finicky and refuse to eat his regular cat

Check for Magnesium

One of the prime considerations in determining the quality of your cat's food is the level of "ash," or mineral magnesium, it contains; this substance has been discovered to be the culprit responsible for development of kidney stones. In males, whether intact or neutered, these stones can block the narrow urethra

and create a life-threatening condition. Virtually all premium cat foods are designed to be low in this stone-causing mineral, but occasionally a cat whose urine is particularly alkaline will require a special veterinary-formulated food that is even lower in ash (usually less than 0.1 percent). Adequate water intake is, again, especially important for these cats to maintain a natural flow of urine.

While many cats are eager to sample from your plate, it's best to limit your cat's diet to specially formulated cat foods.

> **TUNAFISH**
>
> Cats find the strong fishy smell of tuna very appealing, tempting owners to feed it as a special treat or a preferred diet. But feeding a cat a lot of tuna can cause *steatitis*, a condition where vitamin E is destroyed by the excessive amounts of fatty acids in the food. Another potential problem is that the cat may decide it wants a tunafish-only diet, and will turn its nose up at regular cat food. Prevent these problems by feeding only very small amounts of tuna sporadically, as a treat. Make sure it is packed in water, not oil.

Other foods are formulated for geriatric cats, or those who have impaired kidney or liver functions due to age or illness. These foods are generally lower in protein and higher in carbohydrates in order to ease stress on these organs. Cats on this kind of diet should, of course, be carefully monitored by your veterinarian.

Avoid Fad Foods

Vitamin supplementation is unnecessary when a complete and balanced diet is provided. In fact, some added vitamins can have a deleterious effect. In addition, a cat should never be fed dog food. Cats require double the protein and B vitamins as do dogs, which are omnivorous, and a cat needs added amino acids to maintain health. And finally, veterinarians are almost unanimous in their condemnation of trendy vegetarian cat foods, pointing out that the cat is a true carnivore, and that it cannot subsist on the protein contained in vegetables and remain in good health.

Offer your cat fresh water, not milk; most cats are lactose intolerant.

Fish-Flavored Foods

Cats also quickly become spoiled by the stronger smell and flavor of fish-based cat foods. It is wise to avoid these flavors so they can be used successfully to tempt the cat when he is ill, or has been "off his feed." When a cat is sick, he simply will not eat. Especially tempting meals must be offered at that time, because the inappetence will often create a vicious circle. In combination with specially formulated veterinary products that provide the necessary calories for energy to combat illness, those fish-flavored foods can become a lifesaver. Another special treat for a sick cat is strained baby meat, or one of the chicken and noodle dinners available in the baby food section of the grocery store. The soft nature of these baby foods allows you to draw them up into a syringe (without the needle), with which you can feed a cat too weak or reluctant to eat.

Offering Treats

People will be people, and pet owners are suckers for four-footed beggars. And cats will be cats, which means that whatever is on your dinner plate will undoubtedly seem far better than whatever is in your cat's bowl. With a few guidelines and some common sense in mind, it will cause no harm for the occasional "treat" to be offered to the cat. As a rule of thumb, no treat should be offered more than two or three times a week, and should be given only in very small amounts, rather than full meal-sized portions.

READING THE CAT FOOD LABEL

Cats, like people, have certain specific nutritional requirements. For the most part, how well the different cat foods meet these needs has been ascertained through extensive testing by regulatory organizations, most notably the Association of American Feed Control Officials (AAFCO). When choosing a food for your cat, look for this type of statement on the label: "Animal feeding tests using AAFCO procedures." These foods were tested on cats.

When reviewing ingredients, remember they're listed in decreasing order by weight, which means the heavier, more abundant ingredients will be first. These include meats (or fish) and water. Remember, too, that cats are carnivores and must eat meat. They do not do well on a vegetarian diet. Ask your veterinarian or a cat breeder for dietary recommendations.

The thousands of pictures that show cats and kittens eagerly lapping up dishes of milk or cream have probably been responsible for more cats' tummy upsets than anything else. The vast majority of cats are lactose intolerant and should never be offered cow's milk. For a dairy treat, the cat or kitten can be offered small amounts of plain yogurt, cottage cheese or a saucer of goat's milk.

Meat is a favorite of cats; they are, after all, carnivores. A cooked egg, or a tablespoon of ground beef, steak or liver is a special treat. Chicken and fish are nice snacks as well but should be offered only after cooked, and only after any bones have been removed.

Cats should never be allowed to eat chocolate; even a small amount is quite poisonous to animals.

chapter 7

Grooming Your Longhaired Cat

Every cat will benefit from grooming. Every longhaired cat will benefit from daily grooming. Furthermore, every owner will benefit in ways perhaps not even imagined from the act of grooming his or her cat.

Of all the many "old wives' tales" told about cats, probably the most harmful is the one that says a cat shouldn't or needn't be bathed. While most cats have a slight natural aversion to being wet, baths can and should become routine, given at least once every month or two. This can be accomplished at home, at a veterinarian's office or at one of the increasing number of "cats-only" grooming and boarding salons.

The reasons for bathing are numerous. Consider this worst-case scenario: What if your cat is suddenly infested with fleas, or worse yet, rolls in a toxic substance, such as antifreeze? At a time like this,

would you rather deal with a cat that is accustomed to grooming, or with one who is convinced you are inflicting the Chinese water torture with a new twist? So, as this chapter begins, accept as your mantra "I *will* bathe my cat. I *will* bathe my cat."

Before we get to the "B" word, though, we should cover some of the fundamentals of grooming.

The cat's coat, particularly that of a longhair, is designed to protect her from the elements. Naturally secreted skin oils coat the hair to create a fairly efficient water-repelling outer layer. These same skin oils, though, when combined with dead hair, create tangles, mats and an overall unkempt appearance. Additionally, current evidence indicates that the dander formed by a cat's skin is reason for most human allergies to cats. Highly allergic people seem able to tolerate a well-groomed longhair cat much better than one of a shorthaired variety that rarely sees a comb or soapsuds.

Consistency Is Key

Consistent grooming with the correct tools is the most important factor in keeping both cat *and* owner happy. Even if you invest in a monthly trip to the grooming shop, there is still daily maintenance to perform on the longhaired cat. Just five minutes a day, as you are watching television, will make all the difference to you and your cat. When done religiously, on a daily basis, even the most reluctant cat will begin to relax and accept her fate . . . and even begin to enjoy it!

What You'll Need

Of utmost importance is a good metal comb. A Belgian steel comb, which is available at some pet stores (and can probably be ordered for you if not kept in stock), is an investment that will last a lifetime. To determine whether a comb is a good one, hold it up to the light. You want to find no tiny burrs or nicks in the steel. These will pull or snag your cat's hair, and cause pain that will make combing an ordeal rather than a pleasure. This approximately seven-inch basic comb will have one-inch-long teeth that are divided equally between medium-coarse and finer spacing. These long teeth will penetrate the hair and get all the way to the skin to remove the dead hair at its source. A bristled brush is worthless for this purpose, as it cannot get all the way to the skin.

A complete set of grooming tools will also include a shorter, finer-toothed comb (sometimes called a flea comb) for the "finish" work on faces and feet. The same test for burrs by holding it to the light should be given to this comb. Additionally, a curved-wire "slicker" brush, in the smallest size (and softest wire) available, is helpful for smoothing curls in belly hair, and fluffing hair on the feet.

A good comb will be your most important grooming tool.

If your cat is older, and has not been exposed to a grooming regimen, hope is not lost. Gentleness and consistency, however, along with a healthy dose of stubbornness on your part, will be necessary. If, however, this cat's fur has already become matted, do both yourself and your cat a favor—take her to your veterinarian or groomer to be shaved in order to eliminate the mats. Never, ever, subject your cat to yanking and tugging to remove mats; if you do, the cat will then associate you, the comb and grooming sessions with pain. Better to begin fresh, with a manageable, shaved coat, and therefore avoid pitfalls in the future.

The Grooming Procedure

Cats least like to have the underneath and groin areas combed, so this is the area where you should begin. That will leave the easier combing of the back, head

and chest until last, and the grooming session will end—when *you* decide it has ended—on a completely pleasurable note. Cats that are accustomed to grooming can be laid in your lap on their back for the stomach combing; and each leg—in both the front and the rear—should be lifted to comb beneath. For a cat new to the experience, though, it might be easier to use one arm to stretch the cat up to a standing position on her back legs as you reach around with the other arm to comb the stomach, underarms, pantaloons and groin. If the cat has been shaved, it's still a good idea to go through all of these motions every day, to accustom the cat to the feel of the comb, and to your requirement that she submit to this procedure.

Begin by combing your cat's stomach—in time the cat will grow to love it!

If the cat struggles, be gentle but insistent. You may have to stop the combing for a few minutes until she calms down, but never let the cat get away from you. She must learn that these few minutes per day are something that you will require, and that you will "out-stubborn" even the wiliest feline. This does not mean that you should hold the cat down or force her into submission, but rather that you should simply not allow her to go on her way until you are done. To make the process easier, these sessions should ideally be performed by one person so that the cat will not feel trapped, or "ganged up on." Talking to her in a soft voice also helps ease her worries.

Finally, the cat can be situated on her stomach in your lap, where you will continue the comb-through on the back, chest, head and tail. These areas should be easiest, and will quickly become soothing and enjoyable—the "ice cream" treat to end the daily session.

Tackling Tangles

Any time your comb encounters a tiny tangle, or the beginnings of a mat, you should stop. Rather than yanking it out, use the thumb and forefinger of the hand not holding the comb to grasp the tangle as near to the skin as possible. This will keep the comb from pulling excessively. Use only a tooth or two of the comb to separate the tangle into smaller, easier-to-remove sections.

Again, if the mats or tangles become unmanageable, shaving is preferable to pain. Most veterinarians can tell tales of treating cats whose owners have attempted to cut mats out and have accidentally scissored open gaping wounds in their cat's skin.

A special pair of cat claw clippers will make the patience-trying procedure of clipping claws easier.

Tearing Stains

Another daily routine beneficial for all cats, but most importantly for Persians, who may have a tendency to tear because of their large eyes and flat faces, is a face wash. This can be accomplished with just a warm, moist washrag. It is preferable, though, to gently apply boric acid solution with a cotton cosmetic pad to cleanse and soothe the eyes. The fur around the eyes of lighter-colored cats will stain if the tearing or "matter" is allowed to remain.

Clipping Claws

In addition to your daily grooming schedule, a weekly claw clip should be a regular practice. Small scissors with curved ends are available at most pet stores and are made especially for cat claws, but ordinary fingernail clippers will do an adequate job. For this task, take your cat into good light. With one hand use thumb and index finger to apply gentle pressure to the top and bottom of each toe in turn. This pressure causes the claw to extend. Holding it near the light, you can see

the vein that runs down into the claw and ends just before the claw curves. Nip off the tip of each claw (don't forget the back feet!), taking care not to cut into this vein. For novices to claw clipping, having a styptic pencil (available in men's shaving needs areas in drugstores) can be handy in case the vein is accidentally nipped. If this accident occurs, it will be somewhat painful to the cat, and will bleed, but no permanent damage will be done. As with combing, the cat should not be allowed to go on her way until all claws are clipped. This may mean resting between claws if the cat begins struggling.

After a month or two of gentleness, persistence and dedication on your part, even the most irascible cat will learn to relax and at least tolerate—if not actively enjoy—these grooming sessions. Then, you will be ready for the next step . . . the dreaded bath.

Bathing Your Cat

If your cat was obtained from a good breeder, she will have become accustomed to baths as a kitten. Show cats are bathed every week, and kittens learn early that this is just one more part of life. If your Fluffy has never been bathed, though, it might be advisable to have an extra pair of hands at the ready to play "catcher" in case of a sudsy escape.

Bathing is an integral part of your cat grooming regimen.

If you have attended a cat show, and have seen all of the gorgeous longhaired cats, you will have noticed that some have coats poufed so that every hair stands out from the body, yet others have long, silky, flowing coats; there are as many hair textures for cats as there are for people. Some coats have a tendency to be oily, some curly and others flyaway and unmanageable. Some are fine, others coarse; some are dense and others thin. The best groomers have "tricks of the trade" for all these different coat textures, but they cannot possibly all be covered here. What will follow are the best general instructions available for the majority of coat textures.

Preparation and Equipment

Again, preparation and proper equipment are important. Using the kitchen sink for bathing a cat is better than suffering bruised knees and an aching back from leaning over a bathtub. The bathroom does, however, have the advantage of a closed door should the cat happen to escape the tub. An inexpensive rubber hose attached to the faucet will facilitate rinsing; if the cat is overly bothered by the sounds of the spray, the spray-head can be removed, leaving only the flexible hose.

Before beginning, assemble your supplies. You will need:

- Claw clippers;
- A mechanics' hand cleaner (Available in automotive departments, the most common brands are Goop, D&L and Go-Jo. Purchase the kind without added pumice or abrasive ingredient.);
- A tearless pet or baby shampoo;
- Dishwashing liquid;
- A good, all-purpose pet shampoo;
- Vinegar;
- A washrag and two to three towels;
- A hand-held hair dryer (Cats seem to tolerate better those dryers whose motors whine the least, so often the least expensive—and least portable—hand-held dryers are best. If you are buying one specifically for your cat, see if the store will allow you to plug them in to listen to the difference in motor sounds.);
- All of your combs and a slicker brush.

Once your supplies are assembled, you will be ready to reach for your cat, who will undoubtedly have

disappeared totally into some unknown recess of your house after her extrasensory perception warned her that something was afoot.

Once the cat is found, your *very first* order of business will be to clip claws. Allow ample time for the bath so that neither you nor your cat will feel the pressure of being rushed. Approach this project armed with both determination and patience. Your cat will undoubtedly be able to think of at least a dozen places that she would *rather* be than in the sink, but once you begin, there will be no turning back. If it is any consolation, each bath should get progressively easier.

The Actual Bath

Next, put the cat into the sink, but do not turn the water on yet. Begin by working the mechanics' hand cleaner into the dry coat, separating the hair and concentrating on areas with the greatest greasy accumulations—around the ears, down the tail and the hips. Then turn the water on and begin adding a little warm water to the cleaner to work it down through the coat to the skin. Add a little water at a time until it is completely worked through, then rinse. Next, shampoo using your dishwashing detergent, again paying extra attention to those greasy spots, and rinse again. Finally, shampoo with your good, all-purpose pet shampoo. Use the tearless shampoo on a washrag to wash the face and to cleanse the outer portions of the ears.

Persians require more grooming than any other longhaired cat.

The most important step is to rinse, rinse and rinse some more. During the rinsing, use a tablespoon of vinegar in a quart of warm water and pour this over the coat to help cut soap residue. Inadequate rinsing is perhaps the greatest cause of a dry, lifeless coat.

While this shampoo protocol may sound harsh, keep in mind just how efficient the cat's body oils are at "lubricating" the hair. Show cats are bathed in a similar method every single week for an entire show season with no ill effects. If, however, the coat begins to look somewhat dry, you can add a good conditioning cream rinse as a final step.

Using a Dryer

The blow-drying process will also require patience. The better job you do, the better the cat will look when done. Ideally, the cat should not be allowed down until every hair is dry to the feel of your cheek. Your other pair of hands will come in most handy at this stage for holding the dryer and aiming it where needed. If another pair of hands is not available, try rigging some sort of stand to hold the dryer at a convenient height. A stack of towels can serve this purpose.

The whole family can get involved in grooming your cat.

Begin, with the coarsest teeth of your comb, to gently separate the wet hair, combing with the lay of the hair. When it is tangle free and separated, begin lifting the hair with each pass of the comb to allow the air to penetrate underneath the layers. When the hair is almost completely dry, begin combing away from the lay of the hair. Use the fine-toothed comb on the face and legs, and the soft slicker brush to smooth curls out of tummy hair and fluff the hair on the legs.

If Fleas Are Ever a Problem . . .

Now that you are thoroughly comfortable with maintenance grooming and bathing, it's time to face some special problems.

First and foremost, how do you deal with fleas? There are a few isolated areas of the country where fleas are not a major problem—in areas of super-low humidity or of very high altitude. Even those areas are not one hundred percent immune, however. Some new discoveries in the Battle of the Flea may well prove to be the answer to the prayers of millions, especially a new oral medication that interrupts a flea's life cycle by preventing its eggs from hatching. Manufacturer testing and early field results show promising degrees of both efficacy and safety.

Using a flea foam can be an effective means of ridding your cat of fleas.

Other solutions deal with the flea's environment. Good results are reported from people using desiccants, which cause the dehydration and death of fleas by scraping and penetrating their hard exoskeletons. These flea killers work without the use of toxic chemicals that can damage the "good" insects living in your yard, and that can leach into the ground water. These products are best reserved for use in your yard, leaving flea killing in your home up to other products that have a specially manufactured boric acid base.

While flea killers designed for use in the home are not toxic chemicals, they must still be used with care. Boric acid, for instance, can be toxic to cats if ingested in sufficient quantity. A commercial company that applies this product inside your home will use special equipment to pound it deep into carpeted areas and upholstery; this procedure will assure that the chemicals can't be picked up by the cat's fur. Boric acid products should never be applied to noncarpeted or nonupholstered surfaces. For the do-it-yourselfer who wishes to use these products, a heavy yard broom can be used to adequately work them into the carpeting and upholstery.

Despite label directions, the absolutely safest course of action is never to use a flea dip or powder on your cat. Federal guidelines outline which toxic chemicals are and are not safe for cats. Be aware that products that may be safe for your dog are not necessarily safe for your cat. If you do decide to use a flea dip or powder on your pet, read and follow all safety guidelines on the product carefully. Unfortunately, some long-term effects are not determined by safety testing. More than one product has been widely used on pets only to be removed from the market later on as these sometimes deadly effects become evident.

Similarly, my own best advice is not to use a commercial exterminator who applies toxic chemicals to the interior of your home. Even if there are no seemingly ill effects on your cat after the first or second application, the chemicals can build up both in the environment and in the cat's biochemical makeup. Residual exposure to these toxins can ultimately cause damage to the liver and kidneys, or can be carcinogenic, thus shortening your cat's life.

FLEA FACTS

There are no easy answers to flea control, but to beat the bugs, you must first understand flea biology. Adult fleas mate on Kitty and remain there unless involuntarily dislodged. A blood meal stimulates egg laying; ten female fleas can produce 250,000 offspring in thirty days.

Most eggs fall from Kitty into the environment. In one to fourteen days, eggs hatch into tiny, maggotlike larvae. In another three weeks, the larvae spin cocoons, then later emerge as adults. The complete life cycle takes thirty days or less and fleas can live from a few weeks to more than a year. They can survive months without feeding, and can even remain frozen for a year and revive.

Does this mean that your cat will simply have to live with fleas? Absolutely not. Fleas are deadly! They cause anemia by robbing your cat of blood and introduce parasites such as tapeworms. Fleas can and do kill cats.

The best advice is to be an informed consumer, and to discuss with your veterinarian how to handle a flea infestation. New, less toxic and more natural, environmentally friendly products are entering the

market all the time; these can be, at the very least, a starting point in the battle against fleas. Your veterinarian can help you map out a program designed for your specific needs, such as where you live, what other animals you have and whether your cat is indoor only or indoor/outdoor.

Waging the Battle

As these pesky creatures evolve into more and more resistant varieties, often a combination of methods are in order to accomplish complete and lasting eradication. Certainly, the attack should have three points of focus: the lawn, the house and the pets, preferably all at the same time.

Whatever treatment you decide to use on the lawn, it's best to begin by treating the four- to six-foot area around the house, and then work out from there. This "barrier" will prevent fleas in the lawn from escaping into the house as the treatment is being applied. Instead, they will be chased outward, away from the house.

If chemicals are needed inside the house, ask your veterinarian to recommend the safest and most effective brand. For maximum safety, pets should not be in the house during treatment. A trip to the groomer for a professional de-fleaing while the treatment is underway is a good way to use that time.

For the do-it-yourselfer, especially for one with more than one cat, begin by spraying or fogging (with a veterinarian-recommended product) a single room such as a bedroom. This room should be one that can be sealed off from the rest of the house. During this treatment, prevent fumes from escaping into the rest of the house by using masking tape to hold plastic in place over any air-conditioning/heating vents, and by sealing off the door with either masking tape or towels. Leave this room sealed, preferably for twenty-four hours, to provide maximum kill time for any resident fleas. After opening it again, air the room out for several hours.

On the next day, if a groomer is not an option, flea-bathe your pets with a veterinarian-recommended insecticidal shampoo. After each cat is "flea free," put her into the treated room and leave the sealing intact. Once all cats are bathed, and safely ensconsed in their "clean" room with ample food, water and litter, renew the sealing around the door and treat the rest of the house. Follow label directions on either sprays or foggers. One of the most frequent mistakes made when using these products is under-treating; be sure to use enough foggers to treat *under* furniture, *under* sofa cushions and in any other hidden spots.

A well-groomed cat can be quite a sight to see.

When using foggers, err to the side of caution in airing out the premises. Leave the cats in the sealed "clean" room for at least a night; this will prevent them from inhaling any residual fumes or walking on still-moist treated areas.

Because of the rapid life cycle of the flea, this treatment should be repeated every ten days to two weeks, or longer in the case of a particularly serious infestation. Some newer insect growth regulator chemicals that, in effect, sterilize newly hatched fleas, can prevent reproduction and are therefore particularly effective. Because of the different cycles of the flea (egg, larvae, pupae and adult flea), anticipate a minimum of two treatments.

When bathing a cat with fleas, use a cat-safe flea shampoo. Begin around the perimeter of the face, forming a barrier to prevent fleas from trying to escape from the body to the head. Soap the cat from front to back, making sure that suds reach all the way to the

skin. Fleas are known to find even the tiniest patch of skin when it's missed. Once the cat is completely saturated, allow some time for the product to kill (rather than simply stun) the fleas. Use that time to manually remove, with a flea comb, any fleas hiding in the facial hair, around the eyes and in the whisker pads. A small container of the flea shampoo near the sink will allow you to "dunk" any live fleas that come off in your flea comb.

GROOMING SUPPLIES

- Stainless-steel wide-tooth comb
- Curved-wired slicker brush
- Fine-toothed flea comb
- Cat nail clippers
- Flea shampoo
- Baby oil
- Cotton balls
- Commercial ear-cleaning
- Gauze pads
- Saline solution
- Dishwashing liquid
- Mechanic's hand cleaner
- Baby shampoo
- Vinegar
- Washrags or towels
- Hand-held hair dryer
- Rubber-hose spray attachment for faucet

One particularly safe and effective product (California Special, manufactured by Safe-N-Sure Products, Inc.) contains docusate sodium and hendecenoic acid, neither of which is poisonous. It comes in both a shampoo and a dip formulation, both of which should be used on a dry coat (no prewetting). The dip can be used as a premise spray, also. Mix the dip at the recommended concentration, and put it into a squeeze bottle. This will allow you to aim the dip wherever needed to provide the barrier around the face. This product can be safely used even on very young kittens or on pregnant or nursing queens. Leave the wet dip on for five to ten minutes to achieve maximum kill, and then follow with a maintenance bath to remove all residue and to leave the cat looking nicely groomed.

Other Grooming Considerations

The presence of fleas is not the only challenge to be faced when grooming your cat. The following are some problems you should hope never to encounter.

- A cat that gets into motor oil or grease. A good application of mayonnaise, followed by a rinse (or two, if needed), the mechanics' hand cleaner and then a full bath should do the trick.
- A cat that meets the wrong end of a skunk. A thorough soak in tomato juice, followed by the regular bath regimen will eliminate the unpleasant aroma. Pour the tomato juice through the hair and allow it to absorb the skunk's spray for a few minutes before bathing.

After a hard day among the flowers and dirt, your cat will need a good brushing.

- A cat that has gotten into antifreeze. First, submerge the cat in warm water to remove as much of the antifreeze as possible, and to prevent further absorption into the skin. A quick cleansing bath should be followed immediately by an emergency trip to the veterinarian. If the cat has ingested this chemical, it is a life-threatening situation!
- A cat that has walked in tar. Soak your cat's tar-covered paw in a dish of kerosene, and rub the area with your fingers to loosen the tar. Immediately wash the paw well with shampoo to remove all residue of the kerosene, which is toxic.

chapter 8

Your Cat's Health

The cat was long the "poor stepchild" of veterinary medicine. A veterinarian who completed his education some fifty years ago told me that his entire formal veterinary education regarding cats consisted of five words: "This also applies to cats."

The burgeoning popularity of the cat as America's favorite house pet has increased attention to everything from nutrition to vaccinations to treatment for disease and injury. Veterinarians are able to tap the resources of human medicine, and to utilize state-of-the-art techniques, procedures and equipment. With any luck, you won't have to experience firsthand the costs of any serious medical procedures on your cat. As a cat owner, however, you must be prepared to absorb the costs of normal veterinary care, which includes such things as an annual checkup, routine vaccinations, wormings and dental care.

Finding a Veterinarian

When choosing which veterinarian will care for your cat on a regular basis, your selection process should be no less discriminating than it would be when choosing your own doctor. Ask other cat owners in your area for recommendations. You can also call the American Animal Hospital Association at (800) 252-2242. Ask for the Member Service Center, and request a list of any AAHA-approved veterinary clinics in your area. Fewer than fourteen percent of the small-animal hospitals in the United States and Canada are accredited members of AAHA; these members meet high standards in all areas of facilities and care.

Common sense will dictate that the veterinary facilities be clean and properly maintained and that they have complete diagnostic equipment and surgical and pharmaceutical facilities. You should request a tour of the facilities to determine if they meet your expectations. The question of emergency service should be covered—what will happen if your cat becomes ill or is injured during "off" hours? Will the veterinarian be available for after-hours calls, or will you be referred to an emergency clinic? If the latter is the case, will that emergency clinic meet the same standards as your veterinarian's own office?

A FIRST AID KIT

Should your cat ever be injured or become ill, having a first aid kit on hand whill help you provide emergency treatment until you're able to get the cat to a veterinarian. Keep the kit in a cool, dry and easily accessible place. Check the contents periodically to make sure nothing has spilled or leaked, and to replace any medications that are beyond their expiration date.

Adhesive tape (1-inch roll)
Antibiotic eye ointment
Cotton balls
Cotton-tipped applicators
Eyedropper (plastic)
Flashlight
Gauze pads and roll
Hairball remedy (commercial or white petroleum jelly)
Hemostat
Hydrogen peroxide (3 percent)
Kaopectate
Linen cloth, sheet or blanket
Masking tape
Mineral oil
Panalog ointment
Rubber bands (wide—for use as tourniquet)
Scalpel
Scissors (blunt tipped)
Syringe (plastic or glass, 10 cc)
Syrup of ipecac
Teaspoon
Thermometer
Triple antibiotic ointment
Tweezers

Your Kitten's First Visit to the Vet

Your kitten's introductory visit to the veterinarian should include a test for the feline leukemia virus (FeLV) and the feline immunodeficiency virus (FIV). These tests are especially important if you have other cats in your home. Both of these diseases are carried in the bloodstream and cause the kitten to be highly infectious even though he may show no outward symptoms for months, or even years.

This initial visit should also involve a stool check for signs of intestinal parasites. The veterinarian will check internal organs through palpation, check the heart for signs of abnormal rhythm, look into the ears to determine if ear mites are present and into the mouth for evidence of infection.

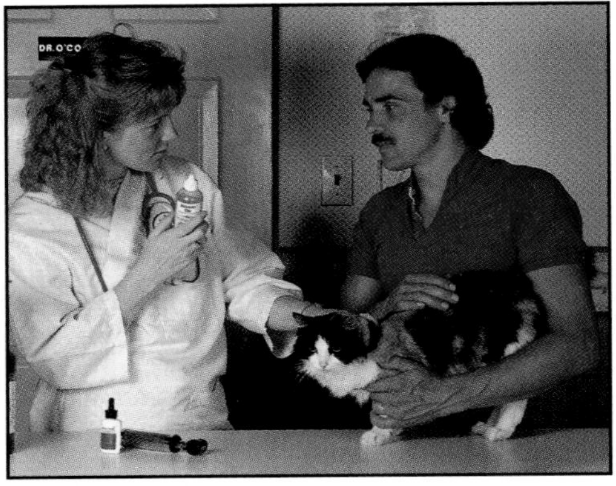

You and your veterinarian will be your cat's first line of defense.

If the kitten has not yet had his first series of immunizations, the veterinarian will give a vaccination for the feline upper respiratory series of viruses. Depending on the kitten's age, the chances of exposure and other factors, the veterinarian may recommend a rabies vaccination (often required by law), and one of the newer vaccinations against FeLV and FIV. These latter two vaccinations are not needed in many cases, and both have caused some controversy in veterinary medical circles due to questions of low efficacy and possible side effects. Discuss the vaccinations thoroughly with your veterinarian in order to make an informed decision.

As a general rule, if the cat is to be indoors only and not exposed to other cats, the FeLV and FIV vaccines are not needed and may expose your pet to unnecessary risks. Hopefully, within the next few years any problems with these vaccines will be fully resolved so that owners can look forward to full, complete and safe protection against these deadly diseases.

If, on that initial visit, your veterinarian finds any signs of illness, the kitten should be returned immediately to the breeder, shelter or pet shop from which he was obtained. Stressing a sick kitten by taking him to a new home, and beginning what may ultimately be very expensive treatment, will be counterproductive to the kitten's welfare and may well void contractual provisions for getting your money refunded. In addition, it would certainly expose any other cats you have at home to unnecessary risk.

By all means, discuss all aspects of your kitten's care with your veterinarian. You should have learned what food the kitten has been reared on; your veterinarian can help you consider the possible options and proper procedure for a change to a more appropriate diet if you decide that one is needed. At this first visit, plans for neutering or spaying should be discussed. Different breeds mature at different rates, but ideally this surgery should be scheduled for a time before the growing kitten's hormones tell him that there is more to life than food and soft human laps. Make sure to schedule future vaccinations and make a note of them.

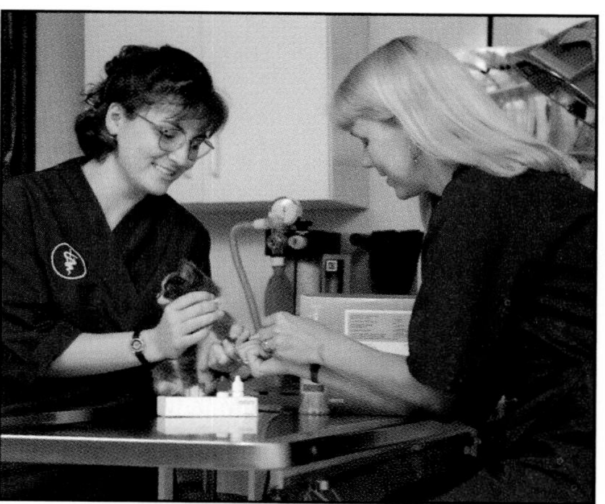

Your kitten should be tested for FeLV on his first visit to the vet.

After the "All-Clear"

An "all-clear" from the veterinarian can be the beginning of a relationship with your kitten that can easily extend twelve to fifteen years or more. You will have prepared your home for the new arrival by "kitten-proofing" it against common hazards; you will be armed with the dedication to train the kitten to

become a well-mannered addition to your family, and you will be providing him with those elements that make for a happy kitten, from appropriate toys and litter box to the best in nutrition.

So, what can be anticipated in future health care?

Declawing

First, of course, is the decision whether to declaw your kitten. Essentially, this surgical procedure should be performed only as a last resort if all training fails; it should never, ever be considered if your cat is to be allowed out of doors. Possible complications include incomplete removal, in which the claw will regrow, often into the foot; infection if the feet are dressed or cared for improperly; and the possibility of temperament changes and behavioral problems. Additionally, while we know of no veterinary studies to support this, there is evidence that declawed cats may suffer more from arthritis in later years.

The surgery, which has been made safer with the advent of new anesthetics and procedures, involves not only the removal of the claw, but also the nail bed and even, in most instances, removal of the first joint of the toe. Only the front claws should ever be removed. It is done under general anesthesia, and the cat's paws will be bandaged for a few days to allow healing. During the healing period, the litter in the cat's box should be replaced by shredded paper to minimize pain.

Neutering or Spaying

The second elective surgery to consider for your cat is neutering or spaying. Every cat that is not intended for a responsible, knowledgeable breeding program of pedigreed cats should be neutered or spayed for social, health and behavioral reasons. The altered cat is less likely to roam, "call" for a mate, fight and mark his territory by "spraying." Contrary to popular opinion, female cats also mark territory by inappropriate urination, though the male's pungent urine is particularly offensive to human noses.

The health benefits of neutering and spaying are well documented, and include lessening the possibility of certain types of cancers. The female that is spayed will not have to face possible cystic ovaries or life-threatening uterine infections.

The surgical sterilization procedure is quick and relatively painless, and the cat can be back to normal within a day if it's a male, and within a few days if it's a female. The male is anesthetized, and a small incision is made in the scrotum, through which the testes are removed. The female's surgery, a ovariohysterectomy, is slightly more complicated, and involves a larger abdominal incision to remove both the ovaries and the uterus.

Myths About Spaying and Neutering

The 1990s have seen the widespread dissemination of educational material debunking some of the more prevalent "old wives' tales" regarding sterilization of cats. The following are some of these myths.

Sterilization is "unnatural." Cats that have been neutered or spayed prior to the hormonal changes of maturation will never miss what they have not experienced. Besides, those hormonal changes can occur as early as five to six months. Most veterinarians recommend that cats be spayed or neutered at five to seven months of age.

A female cat allowed to have a litter will make a better pet. This misinformation has persisted for hundreds of years, but has no foundation in fact. While female cats are wonderful, attentive mothers to their kittens, their personalities prior to having litters are no different from their personalities afterward.

A neutered or spayed cat will become fat and lazy. Again, this myth has no basis in fact. Sterilized barn cats are every bit as efficient at mousing as their intact counterparts. In a pet home, where proper attention is paid to nutrition, the owner can control obesity. Boredom and an improper diet are much more likely than sterilization to cause a cat to become fat and lazy.

A pedigreed cat should be bred. Responsible cat breeders, armed with an impressive knowledge of genetics, heritable traits and lineages, work very hard to perpetuate many beautiful and distinctive breeds of cats. Only the best representatives of a breed, and those which have been certified clear of any genetic anomalies, belong in a responsible breeding program. In other words, simply having papers on a cat does not mean that you should breed your cat. Indiscriminate breeding by uninformed pet owners runs the risk of both producing unhealthy and unsound cats, and of perpetuating any genetic defects that responsible breeders may be trying to eliminate from the breed.

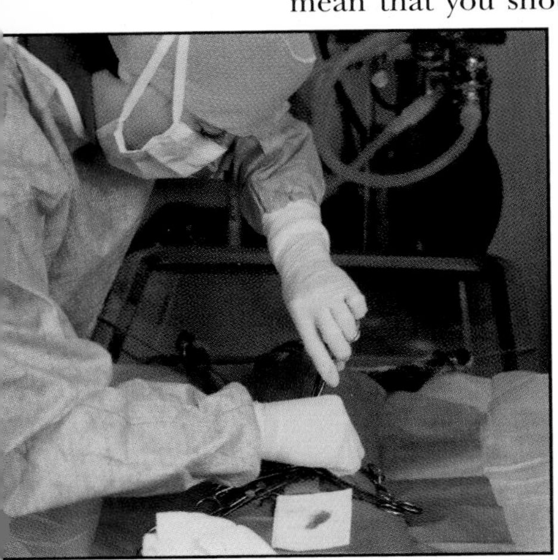

Spaying is a surgery in which the ovaries and the uterus of a female cat are removed.

I can supplement my income by breeding cats and selling the kittens. This bit of misinformation will send breed fanciers into gales of laughter. When done responsibly, the associated costs of a litter will usually far outweigh any income received. Among those costs are the stud fee; veterinary costs prior to breeding, during the pregnancy and for a cesarian section, should it be necessary; the highest-quality food to ensure the health of the mother cat and her kittens; vaccinations for the kittens; and any advertising involved in the sale of the litter.

Infectious Diseases

While they have been covered somewhat in the previous pages, you, as a cat owner, should be aware of the different kinds of infectious diseases cats are vulnerable to, and of the vaccinations available to protect against them.

The normal "kitten shot" will contain protection against the feline upper respiratory series of viruses, including panleukopenia (kitty "distemper"), feline rhinotracheitis and feline calici virus, and may provide vaccination against feline chlamydia. This series is normally given in two injections (or by intranasal administration, depending on the type of vaccine used), two to three weeks apart, and then followed by annual revaccinations. While these vaccinations do not provide one hundred percent protection against all strains of upper respiratory viruses, they have all but eliminated the previous life-threatening nature of these diseases. Vaccinated cats, if exposed, will develop a less serious case of the disease.

Any upper respiratory infection in your kitten or cat should be checked by your veterinarian. Even mild upper respiratory infections can be dangerous, because a kitten or cat that cannot smell won't eat, and can further debilitate because of inappetence. Good supportive care, including force feeding if necessary, can help the cat or kitten overcome most upper respiratory infections.

Three Deadly Feline Diseases

Cat owners have been devastated for many years as they watched their cats sicken and die from one of three diseases that have been fairly recently isolated in the laboratory: feline leukemia, feline immunodeficiency virus (feline AIDS) and feline infectious peritonitis. The three diseases share the following characteristics: All three are viral in nature; the cat may carry any of these viruses in his bloodstream for years before showing symptoms; all three are almost invariably fatal. Researchers have concluded that transmission from one cat to another requires more than casual contact; the viruses are transmitted by infected saliva, blood, feces or urine. Thus, a cat could be infected by sharing water bowls and food dishes with an infected cat, or by being bitten

A healthy appetite is a sign of good health; likewise, avoidance of food usually indicates illness.

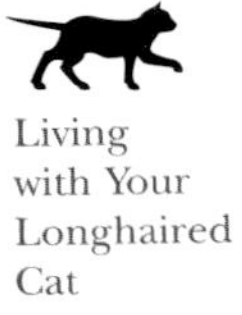

or even groomed by an infected cat. Kittens can also acquire one of these viruses in utero from their mothers or via infected milk. You should take all possible precautions to avoid introducing a new cat that hasn't been tested for these viruses into a household with other, healthy cats. In the case of feline leukemia and FIV, a simple blood test can provide peace of mind.

The Feline Leukemia Virus

As the name would imply, this disease is similar in nature to human leukemia; it attacks the immune system, and was isolated in the 1960s. Studies of cat colonies show that after constant exposure to the disease for twenty weeks, eighty percent of their populations become infected. Environmental stresses such as illness, overcrowding or poor sanitation can contribute to the number of cats that will develop symptoms. The same is true for related diseases caused by a compromised immune system, such as several forms of cancer, FIP, feline infectious anemia and many others. Cats can and do, however, mount an immune response to the original onslaught of this virus, making it possible to develop the resistence needed to overcome it and to lead normal lives.

Veterinary research has provided cat owners with thorough testing tools to determine exposure, and several new vaccines that will aid in protecting those cats at risk. A positive FeLV test on an otherwise healthy cat does not mean a death sentence. Further testing can give insight into the progression of the disease and into the cat's defense mechanisms that are activated in response to exposure.

Feline Immunodeficiency Virus

Otherwise known as feline AIDS, the presence of this disease was only confirmed during the last decade, and was first observed in California. Early cases were thought to be feline leukemia because this disease also attacks the cat's immune system. Primarily transmitted via bite wounds, cats allowed outside are most at risk because they are most likely to get into fights with infected cats. As in the case of human AIDS patients and cats with feline leukemia, FIV-infected cats will likely succumb to a variety of disease-related opportunistic infections. Because infected cats are unable to mount efficient resistance to FIV, mortality is high; infected cats remain infectious for the duration of their lives. Because of the immunosuppressive nature of this disease, a vaccine remains a distant hope. There are, however, efficient tests to determine if a cat is FIV positive, and thus help prevent the unknowing introduction of the disease into a home with other cats. Observing testing protocol, and keeping your cat indoors, will eliminate risk of exposure to this deadly disease.

Feline Infectious Peritonitis

This most frustrating of all cat diseases leaves veterinarians pulling out their hair and cat owners overcome by grief. Despite intensive study, this disease is one about which we still know very little. Researchers tell us that the FIP virus is of the corona virus group, and that it is spread by direct contact among cats. They cannot tell us, however, why the vast majority (seventy-five percent, according to current studies) of those cats exposed never develop any apparent infection, and another large percentage show only mild respiratory infection. Only less than five percent of infected cats develop the secondary and almost invariably fatal disease.

When one cat in a multiple-cat household becomes ill, it is sometimes necessary to isolate him from the others.

Symptoms of the secondary disease manifest in many different ways. The most common is the "wet" form, in which the first symptoms are depression, loss of appetite and weight loss, followed by accumulation of fluid in the abdomen or chest. In the final stages, the cat usually has a high temperature, along with jaundice and dark urine caused by associated liver failure. FIP is

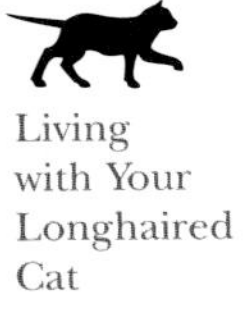

found in cats worldwide, in large cats as well as domestic cats, and usually occurs when the cat is between six months and five years of age, and most often in multiple-cat environments.

Perhaps most frustrating to cat owners, breeders and veterinarians alike is the lack of a definitive serologic test that can determine if a cat is either infected with the virus or is a carrier of it. Likewise, the new vaccine for FIP has received mixed reviews from veterinary researchers. In addition to having a relatively low efficacy rate, there are concerns that the vaccine can precipitate a more virulent and rapid reaction to the disease in cats when they are later exposed to the virus. All factors should be considered when discussing with your veterinarian the advisability of vaccinating your cat.

Transmittable Diseases

Known as zoonotic diseases, these are illnesses that can cross species barriers.

Rabies

The most well known, of course, is rabies. Even though the possibility of your indoor-only cat contracting this disease is minuscule, the safe and effective rabies vaccine is the only sure way to prevent the spread of this terrible killer. There are documented cases of rabid bats and other wildlife biting pet animals after getting into peoples' homes. And even the most careful owner cannot guarantee that his cat might never slip out through a cracked door or window, and thus be exposed to rabies.

Toxoplasmosis

Blamed for birth defects in human children, this intestinal parasite is a protozoan disease that cats can acquire from eating infected birds or rodents, or by ingesting oocysts in contaminated soil. There is the possibility that a person can be infected by handling a cat's litter box without proper sanitary precautions. A pregnant woman should wear disposable plastic gloves when changing a cat's litter box and dispose of the litter carefully. She should also wear gloves when gardening.

Studies show that people are actually much more likely to contact toxoplasmosis from eating raw or undercooked pork, beef, mutton or veal that contain the organisms, than from exposure to cat waste. In fact, about half of the human adult population shows serologic evidence of past exposure. Humans and adult cats rarely show symptoms of infection by toxoplasmosis, but kittens especially can display signs that include fever, lethargy, loss of appetite, weight loss, diarrhea, coughing or difficulty breathing. You can prevent your cat from being exposed to this disease by keeping him indoors and feeding him commercial diets.

Fungal Infection

Commonly known as **ringworm,** the cat is the ideal host for this nonfatal, but annoying disease. The name "ringworm" comes from one form of fungal infection that typically has the appearance of a spreading circle with hair loss and scaly skin at the center and a red ring on the margin. Other fungal infections can attack virtually any area of a cat's skin, including his ears and claws.

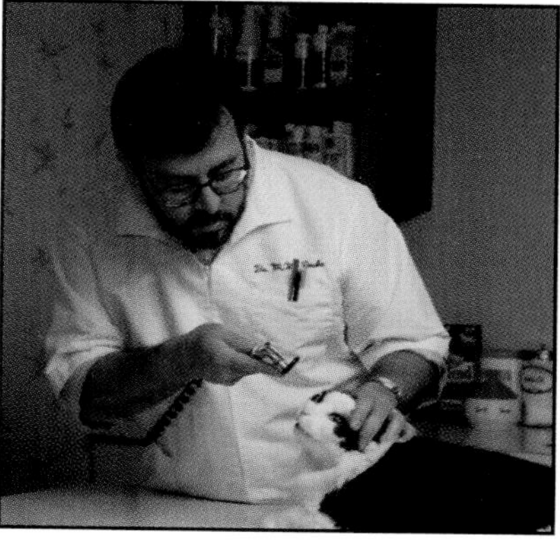

A regular checkup by a vet is vital to your cat's health.

Fungal spores are airborne, and can live off a host for about eight months. Even an indoor cat is not completely safe from spores being tracked in on shoes, or even floating in through open windows. People can also receive outside exposure, become infected and transmit the fungus to their cats. Both cats and people can harbor an inapparent (asymptomatic) fungal infection.

A cat's best defense against fungal infection is a healthy immune system not stressed by other diseases, and benefits of good care and nutrition. Upon exposure, this cat can mount an effective response. If, however,

your cat shows scaly or scabby patches of skin, a trip to your veterinarian is in order.

If a fungus is confirmed, the veterinarian will likely prescribe an internal (oral) medication as well as a topical ointment or cream with which to treat the patches. If infection is widespread, the veterinarian may also recommend using a dip on the cat. The most effective kind is a lime-sulfur dip that, because of its extreme odor, the owner will likely prefer to be used at the veterinarian's office. This dip should be repeated three times at five- to seven-day intervals. The veterinarian may also recommend shaving the cat in order to remove spores contained within the hair. Be sure to ask him or her about the best procedure for eliminating the fungus from your house.

Parasitic Diseases

Roundworms

Toxocara cati, better known as roundworms, is the most common intestinal parasite found in cats. Adult worms are long and slender, have a spaghetti-like appearance and can be found in the stool of an infected cat. Once present, the worms can migrate into the bloodstream and to other organs in the cat's body; this dangerous condition can be fatal. If they enter the bronchioli and trachea, they can be coughed up by the cat; if reingested, the worms are then introduced back into the cat's stomach.

Cats can become infected by eating or coming into contact with contaminated feces (dog feces can also contain roundworm eggs), by ingesting rodents or other intermediate hosts and by nursing on an infected queen's milk. Because of this ease of infection and the widespread occurrence of this parasite, infection is common. Diagnosis is made by fecal examination, and treatment involves one of several oral medications that your veterinarian can prescribe, all of which are extremely safe and effective. Depending upon the type of medication and the severity of infection, several doses may be required to eliminate roundworms in all stages of their development.

TAPEWORMS

The second most common intestinal parasite is the tapeworm. Your first clue that your cat may have a tapeworm infestation is the discovery of small, elongated, ricelike segments, either in the cat's stool or clinging to the hair around the anus. These segments are broken-off parts of the tapeworms' bodies.

The most common means of tapeworm infestation is the ingestion of fleas that carry the parasite. Any time your cat has fleas, you should be alert for signs of tapeworms. Often, adult tapeworms in a cat's intestinal tract do not cause clinical signs; however, diarrhea following or during a flea infestation should be considered a possible sign of infection. If left untreated, tapeworms can cause a cat to be nutritionally deprived, and to become thin, with a rough, unkempt coat.

Infection by tapeworms can be assumed by the presence of the ricelike segments, or can be determined on fecal examination by your veterinarian. Treatment is safe and effective, and can be either an injectible or oral medication. Reinfestation is likely to occur, however, unless all fleas are eliminated from the cat's environment.

HEARTWORM

While not as common in cats as it is in dogs, heartworm infection can and does occur, especially in the more temperate climates that are prime for the parasite's intermediate host, the mosquito. Cats that are kept indoors are less likely to be bitten by the heartworm-carrying mosquito. Cats in general have a greater immunologic responsiveness to this parasite than dogs do. When cats are infected, treatment for the parasite is usually not needed; rather, symptoms are treated as they occur. Veterinarians rarely recommend a routine preventive medication for heartworm because the risk of this disease in cats is so low.

Arthropod Infestations

FLEAS

The most prevalent of arthropods, of course, is the flea. Although the elimination of fleas was already covered in Chapter 7, it warrants repeating here. To successfully eliminate fleas, a three-pronged approach is necessary: (a) treat the cat; (b) treat the home; and (c) treat the lawn. Fleas can literally be deadly to your cat. They carry a host of infections, most notably tapeworms. Some other diseases, such as feline infectious anemia, are thought to be spread by fleas as well. A severely infested cat can become so debilitated by the consequent loss of blood that anemia often results, thus preventing the cat's immune system's ability to ward off any of a host of other diseases. Fleas should never be taken lightly, and all efforts to eliminate them should be vigorously pursued. Read Chapter 7 on grooming and consult with your veterinarian to develop your plan of attack without delay.

EMERGENCY SYMPTOMS

The following are symptoms the cat owner should be aware may indicate a life-threatening condition. Observation of any of these means that the owner should seek immediate veterinary attention from the cat's regular veterinarian or, if necessary, an emergency clinic.

Inability to urinate (male cats)

Dyspnea—difficulty breathing, including any open-mouthed breathing.

Cyanosis—turning blue, usually first observed in the mouth and gums.

Sudden paralysis

Profuse bleeding

Uncontrollable vomiting

Major trauma—involving lacerations or fractures

Seizures—the cat going rigid, into convulsions, salivating or involuntary urination

Ocular emergencies—any sudden or major problem involving the eye

Kittens suddenly not eating

Disorientation—the cat becoming weak and beginning to stagger

EAR MITES

Found throughout the world, the ear mite, or *Otodectes cynotis*, commonly infests the external ear canals of dogs, cats, foxes, raccoons, ferrets and other carnivores. They are easily spread from one animal to another; if one cat in a multiple-cat household is discovered to have ear mites, it is very likely that all the cats will also be infected. All of them should be treated, regardless of the evident severity of their individual infestations.

Ear mites stimulate inflammatory responses in the ear canal, and then feed on the inflammatory products and secretions. The first indications of an infestation of ear mites are head shaking, ear scratching or a visible accumulation of brown/black debris in the ear mixed with an overaccumulation of oil.

Numerous effective treatments are available from your veterinarian to rid your cat of ear mites. These include an injectible medication as well as topical, oil-based medications that contain a mild insecticide. Before treating the ears for mites, thoroughly clean the ears to remove accumulated debris. A few drops of warm mineral oil should be instilled into the ear to loosen this debris, and cotton swabs used to gently remove it. Never push the swabs far into the ear canal; doing so can rupture the ear drum, and can also push the mites and debris further into the ear canal, making them even more difficult to remove. Follow this cleaning procedure prior to each administration of the ear mite medication. To prevent reinfestation, other pets in the household should be checked for ear mites, and treated as well.

Take note of any changes in your cat's behavior; they may be clues to an otherwise unseen illness.

Skin Mites

The most frequently found skin mite in cats is the *Cheyletiella* mite. Some species of this mite are most commonly found in cats, others in dogs and others in rabbits. Adult mites live in the surface of the skin, and result in a condition similar to notoedric mange. Many cats are infested with skin mites, but do not have the "allergic" type response that causes visible lesions. Instead, the owner may notice only an accumulation of what looks like dandruff. Under a veterinarian's microscope, this dandruff will appear to move, thus its nickname, "walking dandruff."

Infested cats, whether they have lesions or not, are infectious, and can infect other cats as well as their

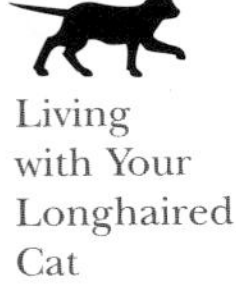

owners. Humans who are sensitive, or "allergic" to these mites, respond in a similar way to being bitten by common lawn chiggers, showing a small, localized, highly itchy raised lesion in the skin. Oftentimes the human's reaction is the first clue that a cat may be infested.

Treatment involves an insecticidal dip provided by or done by your veterinarian. Lime-sulfur dip is highly effective if repeated three times at five- to seven-day intervals. An insecticidal treatment for the home, such as a flea fogger, will eliminate the mites from the household environment.

Eye Problems

Some of the longhaired breeds of cat, most specifically the Persian, have been bred to have larger, more prominent eyes than other breeds. This distinction can create some special health considerations. Even cats without the larger eyes, though, can be sensitive to injury, environmental contaminants, or caustic substances.

The cat depends upon his eyesight as his chief means of stalking and hunting. His vision is particularly acute, even in poor light conditions, but contrary to popular opinion, he cannot actually "see in the dark." The cat's pupils respond by expanding and contracting to compensate for light and to bring objects into clear focus. The third eyelid, or nictating membrane, cleanses and lubricates the eye, compensating for the fact that the cat seldom blinks. Injury to the eye or illness is often first evident as a swelling or redness in this third eyelid. Any change in the normal look of a cat's eye should alert you to investigate the cause.

Discharge

Abnormal eye discharge, particularly discharge that is thick, sticky or mucus- or puslike, suggests a problem. Excessive tearing, squinting and avoidance of light are also signs of a problem. More serious eye problems are suggested when the eye is cloudy or lacks transparency, or when the cat rubs his eyes excessively. Any evidence of this sort, as well as a suspected eye injury, requires prompt veterinary attention. The veterinarian will probably prescribe an ointment or a drop to be instilled in the eye several times a day. Administer this treatment by gently pulling out the lower lid and then putting the medication into the "cup" formed between the lid and the eye.

Tearing

The Persian's tendency to tear more than other cats has been attributed to its relatively shorter nose and flatter face. In actuality, the tearing is caused by a "crimping" of the tear duct, where the pooling space at the inner corner of the eye is too small. This can result in unsightly staining of the face from excessive drainage, but is not indicative of illness. Persian owners can lessen the staining by washing the eye area daily with a pad soaked in boric acid solution, and by minimizing atmospheric pollutants such as dust and smoke. As with daily grooming, a Persian owner must be dedicated to cleanliness in order to fully enjoy the beauty of his or her cat. It is reassuring, however, that responsible Persian breeders have been successfully selecting for cats with a broader-spaced eye to compensate for and to relieve this "crimping."

HOUSEHOLD CHEMICALS THAT ARE DANGEROUS FOR YOUR CAT

automotive de-icers
denture cleaners
deodorants
detergents
drain cleaners
dry cleaning fluids
fertilizer
fireworks
fire extinguisher
fuels
furniture polish
gasoline
glues and adhesives
laundry bleach
matches
metal cleaners
oven cleaners
paint removers
perfumes
photographic developers
pine oil disinfectants
radiator cleaners
rock salt (used for thawing)
rubbing alcohol
shampoos
shoe polish
suntan lotion
styptic pencils

Oral Problems

One of the more important and less scrupulously attended to needs of the cat is proper attention to his teeth and mouth. Recent studies are at odds over the tartar-removing capabilities of a dry-food diet.

Regardless of its effectiveness, however, the simple fact that a cat is fed dry food does not mean that he should not receive regular dental examinations and care.

By far, the dental credo of "an ounce of prevention is worth a pound of cure" holds equally true for cats as it does for humans. Most veterinarians recommend an annual dental checkup and cleaning. As the cat ages, some extractions may be necessary. Rest assured that even some totally toothless elderly cats seen to have no problem eating and maintaining their otherwise robust health.

It's important not to forget about your cat's teeth.

A proper bite is key to a cat's dental health. The kind of bite a cat has is determined by how the upper and lower incisor teeth meet when his mouth is closed. In a level bite, the incisors meet. In the scissors bite, the upper incisors may overlap slightly but still touch the lower incisors. Anything other than a level bite is considered a malocclusion (an improper meeting of the upper and lower teeth), including a bite that is off center, or crooked. An "overshot" bite is one in which the upper jaw juts over the lower jaw, causing the teeth to overlap without touching. An "undershot" bite is the reverse, with the lower jaw projecting beyond the upper, and often resulting in a protrusion of the lower canines from the mouth. Any of these malocclusions can result in premature tooth loss and periodontal problems. All are heritable and genetic in nature.

Bite problems such as these have plagued Persians, and other breeds for which the Persian is the parent breed, for many years. Show standards demand that a cat with a crooked bite be disqualified, and responsible breeders will neither breed nor sell for breeding a cat that has an incorrect bite. These genetic malocclusion problems are slowly but surely being eliminated from the breed.

Allergies

Cats can and do suffer from an array of allergies that rival even those of their human companions. As a reaction caused by the cat's own immune system, an allergy can manifest as a skin rash; as red, watery eyes; as asthma-type breathing difficulties; or as intestinal upsets such as vomiting and diarrhea. Discovering the triggering allergen can be an extremely frustrating process for the cat owner, and has given rise to a whole new specialty in veterinary medicine.

One of the most common allergies is a contact-dermatitis allergic reaction to insecticidal flea collars. This allergy involves hair loss and red, itchy bumps that can become purulent sores in the area under the collar and in surrounding tissue. Flea powders can cause an even more generalized reaction over the entire body of the cat. Just as cats can be very allergic to the chemicals used to combat fleas, they can be equally allergic to bites from the fleas themselves. Flea bite dermatitis is a common reaction to infestation by fleas.

PLANTS THAT ARE DANGEROUS FOR YOUR CAT

House plants: Daffodil, oleander, poinsettia, dumb cane, mistletoe, philodendron, caladium, amaryllis, elephant ear

Flower garden plants: Delphinium, monkshood, foxglove, iris, lily of the valley

Vegetable garden plants: Rhubarb, spinach, tomato vine, sunburned potatoes

Ornamental plants: Oleander, castor bean, daphne, golden chain, rhododendron, lantana

Trees and shrubs: Cherry, peach, oak, elderberry, black locust

Other common chemicals and substances that can cause contact dermatitis include shampoos, poison ivy, poison oak and chemicals used in the environment (such as acids, alkalis, detergents, solvents, soaps and petroleum by-products). Some cats are highly allergic

to the use of fabric-softener dryer sheets on their bedding, and can develop several asthmatic symptoms from close proximity to this allergen.

Cats can be allergic to certain foods, or to substances within the foods. Symptoms range from vomiting and diarrhea to sneezing, swelling of the eyelids and a runny nose. Milk, cheese and fish account for the majority of food allergies.

While medications exist to treat the symptoms of allergies, it is far better and wiser to do intensive detective work to determine the source of the allergen and to remove it, if possible.

Anticipating a curious cat's behavior and preventing it can save both you and your cat trouble in the long run.

Emergency Situations

Poisons and Other Toxic Substances

Cats are far more sensitive to a variety of toxic substances than either humans or dogs. While a cat that is allowed out of doors is always at risk of ingesting or of coming into contact with such deadly substances as rat bait, toxic plants or industrial chemicals such as antifreeze, the indoor-only cat can face equally deadly dangers. You should be fully familiar with the large list of common household plants and substances that can poison a cat. Note the sidebars that list many of the most common poisonous substances. These poisons can cause both acute and insidious, delayed reactions. The latter will usually cause organ failure.

Indoor hazards can, of course, include applications of chemical insecticides to the premises. Even if the cat is removed from the premises until the insecticide is dry and the room is aired out, fumes contained within the carpet or upholstery can still create problems for a cat.

Certain common house plants can be deadly or, at the least, an irritant if ingested by the cat. Some common household disinfectants, such as those containing petroleum products, can over time produce a cumulative toxic effect.

Other common household chemicals are caustic in nature, and if licked or walked through by the cat, can cause burns to the tongue, eyes or skin. Such substances, too, should be quickly washed off before taking the cat to the veterinarian.

Signs of Toxic Poisoning

Signs of acute toxic poisoning can include acute abdominal pain, mouth irritation, drooling, violent vomiting, diarrhea, seizures and coma. If you suspect any of these symptoms may have been caused by poisoning, immediate veterinary attention for your cat should be sought. If the symptoms occur immediately following direct application of a dip or insecticidal spray or powder, take a few moments to wash the offending substance off the cat and to wrap him in a warm towel for the trip to the veterinarian. If possible, bring the flea killer, or whatever the poison happens to be, with you. Knowing what the poison is will help the veterinarian treat your cat more effectively.

A hairball remedy, or just plain petroleum jelly, is a good item to have in your first aid kit.

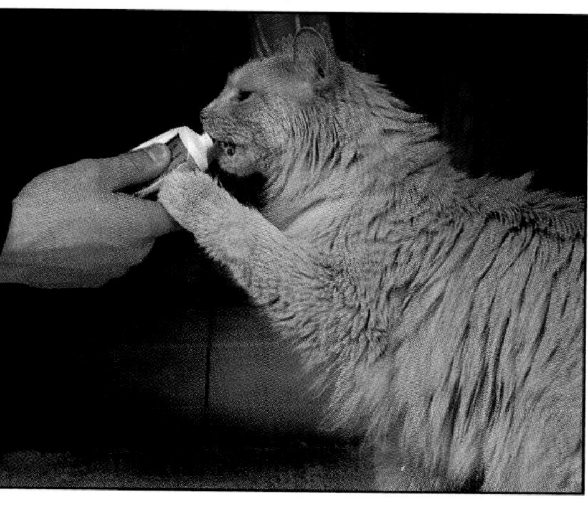

The University of Illinois operates a service called "Toxicology" Hotline for Animals, which can be reached at (217) 333-3611 twenty-four hours a day, seven days a week. You can also call the Animal Poison Control Center at (800) 548-2423. These services can help you care for your cat in an emergency when veterinary treatment is not available.

WHEN TO CALL YOUR VETERINARIAN

In any emergency situation, you should call your veterinarian immediately. You can make the difference in your cat's life by staying as calm as possible when you call and by giving the doctor or assistant as much information as possible before you leave for the clinic. That way, your veterinarian will be able to take immediate, specific action to remedy your cat's situation.

Emergencies include acute abdominal pain, suspected poisoning, burns, frostbite, dehydration, shock, abnormal vomiting or bleeding, and deep wounds. You should also consult your veterinarian if your cat has a thick discharge from eyes or nose, is coughing or sneezing, refuses food, or has a change in bathroom habits. Never give your cat human medication unless instructed to do so by your veterinarian.

You are the best judge of your cat's health because you live with and observe her every day. If you notice changes—such as lethargy, which may indicate a fever caused by infection—don't hesitate to call your veterinarian. Normal cat temperature is 101–102.5 degrees; anything higher indicates illness.

First Aid for Your Cat

It's a good idea to discuss the contents of a first aid kit for your cat with your veterinarian. This kit can be a lifesaver; it can provide you with the means with which to stabilize your cat long enough to get him to a veterinarian (a tourniquet to stop the flow of blood, for example), and can also be valuable in other, smaller mishaps. It can even save an unnecessary visit to the vet. The most important things to include are listed in the "First Aid Kit" sidebar.

You should also discuss with your veterinarian some common medications to keep on hand. Keep in mind that most pain-relieving or fever-reducing analgesics can be deadly to cats. Aspirin, acetaminophen (Tylenol) and phenylbutazone should never be used without your veterinarian's okay. Some medications that your veterinarian might recommend keeping, however, are: Kaopectate (for diarrhea), mineral oil (forconstipation), Panalog ointment (for minor cuts or lesions), syrup of ipecac (to induce vomiting in a cat that has ingested poison), a soothing or antibiotic eye ointment (for irritated or inflamed eyes) and a hairball remedy. Be sure to keep a list of all the medications your veterinarian recommends, along with the appropriate dosages, in your first aid kit.

Artificial Breathing and Heart Massage (CPR)

Artificial breathing is a method by which air is exchanged in an unconscious cat. Heart massage is used to make the heart beat artificially when no heartbeat can be felt or heard. When both these procedures are combined, it is called cardiopulmonary resuscitation, or CPR. Once a cat has stopped breathing, his heart will soon stop beating as well. CPR is the most effective way to try to reverse this life-threatening situation. Always seek veterinary attention when a situation like this one arises, even if your cat begins breathing again.

It's a good idea to make sure you know how to perform these life-support techniques before they're ever necessary. Begin by asking yourself a few questions in order to determine whether either or both procedures are called for:

Is the cat breathing? Look for the rise and fall of the cat's chest. Place your cheek next to the cat's nose and mouth and feel for air.

If *yes,* pull the cat's tongue forward to clear the airway. Observe.

If *no,* feel for pulse.

Does the cat have a pulse? Check this by feeling for the femoral artery, which is located in the groin.

If *yes,* perform artificial breathing.

If *no,* perform CPR.

Artificial Breathing (Mouth-to-Nose Breathing)

1. Lay the cat on a flat surface with his *right* side down.

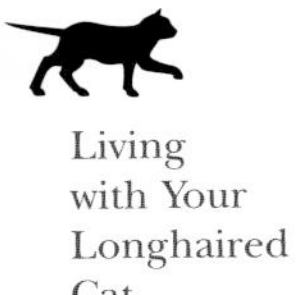

2. Open the mouth and remove any obstructions. Pull the tongue forward and close the mouth again.
3. Place your mouth over the cat's nose and breathe gently into the nostrils. The chest should expand. Remove your mouth to let the air come back out. Do not cover the cat's lips; excess air escapes through the mouth and prevents overinflation of the lungs and overdistension of the stomach.
4. If the chest does not expand, increase the force of your breath into the cat's nose, or lightly cover the cat's lips.
5. You should breathe into the nose once every four or five seconds.
6. Continue until the cat is breathing on his own, or as long as the heart continues to beat.

CPR (Artificial Breathing and Heart Massage)

1. Proceed with mouth-to-nose breathing as described above.
2. Place your fingers and thumb of one hand on either side of the sternum, the bottom part of the rib cage felt just behind the elbows.
3. Compress the chest by pressing fingers and thumb firmly together. Do so six times and then administer a breath. Repeat, one breath for every six compressions. (If possible, continue to massage the heart while administering the breaths.)
4. Pause every two minutes for ten to fifteen seconds. Check for a pulse and spontaneous breathing.
5. Continue the procedure until the heart beats and the cat breathes on his own, or until no heartbeat has been felt for thirty minutes.

Emergency Situations

Shock Signs of shock include semiconsciousness or unconsciousness, confusion and weakness, combined with rapid and/or shallow panting. Place your cat on his side and extend his head to allow for easier breathing. Open the cat's mouth and pull the tongue forward to open the airway as much as possible. Cover him with a towel (but not so much as to cause him to become overheated) and seek veterinary attention.

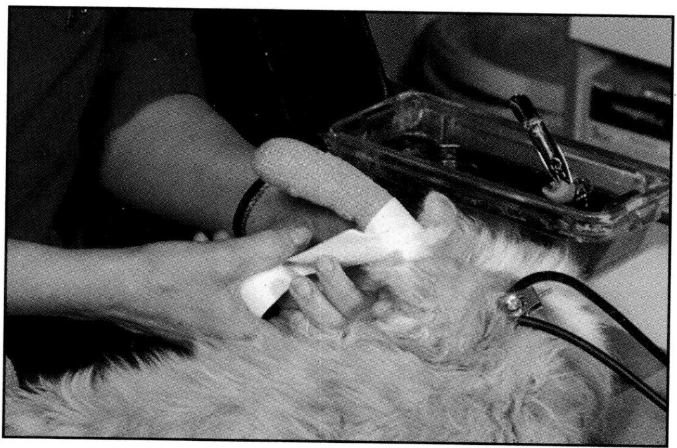

A cat with a broken bone will need emergency treatment.

Trauma Internal injuries and back trauma are most frequently caused by car accidents and falls. To prevent further injury, move your cat as little as possible. Slide him onto a flat, rigid surface, such as a cookie sheet or a large clipboard. Restrain the cat on the surface by wrapping a towel loosely around the cat and the board. Restraining the cat's movement will help prevent simple broken bones from becoming more serious. Seek veterinary attention.

Bleeding Attempt to stop the flow of blood by placing a gauze compress or a clean washrag on the wound and applying pressure. If blood soaks through, don't change the compress; just add another on top of the first one. Continue to apply pressure and take your cat to the veterinarian.

Burns If your cat has burned himself by coming into contact with a hot surface or a flame, apply cold water to the affected area for five minutes. If you can't immerse the area (if the cat has burned his face, for instance), soak a washrag in ice water, wring it out and apply it gently to the burned area. Treat chemical

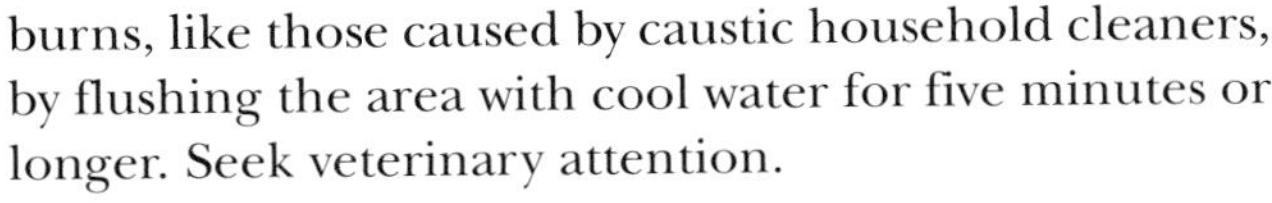

burns, like those caused by caustic household cleaners, by flushing the area with cool water for five minutes or longer. Seek veterinary attention.

Drowning Help expel water from your cat's lungs by grasping him by the hind legs with one hand, and at the nape of the neck with the other; turn him upside down. Give the cat several brisk shakes, or even several rapid downward swings. If the cat still has no pulse and is not breathing, begin CPR as directed above. Veterinary attention is required, especially since inhalation of water can freqeuently result in pneumonia.

A cat who has experienced trauma of some sort will likely have to be x-rayed.

Snake bites If you suspect that your cat has been bitten by a snake, first try to determine whether the snake was poisonous. If possible, kill the snake.

Bites from nonpoisonous snakes generally do not cause pain or swelling. The teeth marks from this kind of bite are horseshoe-shaped, with no evidence of puncture wounds (fang marks). A nonpoisonous snake has round, not elliptical, pupils. If all evidence indicates that the snake was nonpoisonous, treat the bite as a wound, as described below, and take the cat to a veterinarian.

The bite of a poisonous snake also is horseshoe-shaped, but shows evidence of puncture wounds from the two fangs in the upper jaw. The wound will show severe swelling and redness, and will be excrutiatingly painful. The eyes of a poisonous snake generally have an elliptical, not round, pupil.

If you decide that your cat has been bitten by a poisonous snake, and you are within thirty minutes of a veterinary hospital, take the cat there at once. If veterinary treatment is more than thirty minutes away, do the following:

1. *Keep the cat still.* Movement will only cause the venom to circulate faster.
2. If the bite is on a leg, apply a constricting bandage between the bite and the cat's heart. The bandage should be tight, but still loose enough for you to get a finger beneath it. Loosen this bandage for five to ten minutes every hour.
3. *Do not* attempt to wash the wound, apply ice to it, or suck the venom out. After bandaging the cat, proceed immediately to a veterinary hospital.

Wounds All wounds should be thoroughly cleansed with hydrogen peroxide, and then treated with an antibiotic ointment. These wounds, even if minor, should be monitored during the healing process to note the possible formation of an abcess. This monitoring is particularly important in the case of bite wounds inflicted by another cat. Bacteria lurking in a cat's teeth can create terrible abcesses in even minor wounds.

To prevent a cat from reopening a wound on his body, or from causing further damage by licking or scratching head wounds, an Elizabethan collar (named for the high neck ruff that ladies wore during the reign of Queen Elizabeth) can be useful. A homemade one can be fashioned from cardboard cut to an approximately twelve inch circle. In the middle of the circle, cut a hole big enough to fit snugly around the cat's neck but without binding. Cut a slit through from the outside edge to the inner circle so that it can be fitted onto the cat, and then tape it closed. Be sure to

HAIRBALLS

To cats, grooming is a way of life. They are clean creatures who use their specially designed tongues to both keep their hair and skin debris-free and to cover themselves with scent. Hairballs are accumulations of the loose fur the cat swallows as it grooms. This fur either travels through the cat's digestive system and is defecated, or it irritates the system and is vomited out.

You can help keep hairballs to a minimum by combing out your cat's loose hair. If she becomes constipated anyway, you can put a small amount of petroleum jelly on her paws to lick off (cats like the taste). But with regular combing from you and regular grooming by them, cats can handle their hairballs naturally. Anything unusual should be reported to your veterinarian.

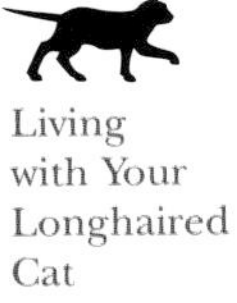

notice whether your cat is eating and drinking properly while wearing one of these collars; it may be necessary to remove it for feeding times, and then replace it.

The Geriatric Cat

Arthritis, rheumatism, cancer, cataracts, strokes, heart disease, failing kidneys—all those geriatric problems to which humans fall victim—can also be found in the geriatric cat. As with humans, the cat's "golden years" can be made pleasant and worthwhile with only a few alterations in lifestyle. While not too many years ago the life expectancy of the cat was less than ten years, the average house cat now lives fifteen years. It is not uncommon for cats to live eighteen to twenty years, and some rare cats go on to twenty-five and beyond.

An older cat should be given special allowances and extra care.

Cats age at different rates due to many factors, including genetic predisposition, nutrition, disease and environmental stresses. Perhaps even more so than in humans, illness, surgery or injury in the geriatric cat can cause accelerated breakdown of his organs. Older cats become more sedentary, and usually seek out warm spots in which to sleep for extended periods of time. Joint stiffness or arthritis is common, as is failing eyesight. It becomes more important than ever for the owner of the geriatric cat to "tune in" to unusual behavior; possible signs of serious illness must not be overlooked, or mistakenly attributed to "just old age." That annual veterinary checkup assumes even more importance. Some of the infirmities of the normal aging process can be eased with something so simple as a veterinarian-recommended change in diet or medication.

The loss of a cat can cause very real grief for owners; counseling is offered by many humane societies.

Loss of muscle tone goes hand in hand with a decrease in physical activity. Both of these result in joint stiffness, especially when the cat awakens from a nap. You can encourage moderate exercise to help compensate for this, by setting aside a short period of time each day to play with your cat at his favorite game—chasing a wadded piece of paper, or following a toy attached to a string. Your cat should not, however, be pressed into activity that overtires him, and for cats with cardiac problems, some activity should be avoided.

Keeping the longhaired geriatric cat clean becomes even more important,since skin can become a problem as the cat becomes less able to cope with self-grooming. If the regular bathing regimen becomes too stressful, there are dry shampoos on the market that help minimize excess skin oils and help keep the cat looking and feeling cleaner. Parasites, such as fleas, become even more deadly to the older or debilitated cat.

If you notice that your cat displays increased thirst and more frequent urination, you should seek veterinary

care. These are often the first signs of kidney failure or of the onset of diabetes, both of which can respond favorably to a change in diet. Constipation is another sign that should be mentioned to your veterinarian, and which can be controlled with simple changes in diet and care.

As a cat becomes less active, his natural tendency to become obese must be scrupulously avoided; excess weight places stress on all of the cat's internal organs. Your veterinarian can help choose the right diet for your elderly cat's changing needs.

Just as obesity in the older cat is a danger, rapid or progressive weight loss can be indicative of something more serious. On the other hand, it could be the result of something so common as dental or periodontal problems and can be remedied. Any noticeable weight loss should, however, be reported to your veterinarian.

Time to Say Goodbye

The most difficult time for a cat owner to face is when the quality of his or her cat's life has become so poor due to infirmities or debilitating illness that the only kind thing to do is save him further pain. The owner, alone, must be the ultimate judge of when that time is, and should approach the decision with the cat's needs as the primary consideration. Age and infirmity alone do not mean that your cat cannot enjoy a sunny spot or affection from you, but if he is suffering from a painful or progressive condition from which there is no hope of relief, then the final and ultimate act of love and kindness is to allow him a painless and dignified death. This is accomplished by an intravenous injection designed for this purpose to be totally painless and nearly instantaneous. Some caring and sympathetic veterinarians will, if asked, make a house-call to provide this service in the cat's accustomed surroundings.

Many humane societies and SPCAs currently offer grief counseling; society has discovered how intense the pain of the loss of a beloved pet can be. A sense of closure can be gained from this type of counseling, or from a family memorial service in which family members can say goodbye to their cat in a way that acknowledges the pet's importance.

(The author would like to thank Dr. Kent Cooper, D.V.M., of Carrier Animal Hospital in Grand Prairie, Texas, for reviewing, advising and giving input on the writing of this chapter.)

part three

Enjoying Your Cat

chapter 9

Feline Behavior and Training

It is a constant source of amazement that people maintain the opinion that cats cannot be trained! As with any species' young—human, canine, feline—a kitten must learn what is and what is not allowable behavior in her home. A pet's behavior is the single most frequently listed cause of pet abandonment at shelters. The owners have either not taken the time or have not learned how to teach their pets proper house manners.

The most frequent behavior problems in cats actually result from instincts, so a certain amount of patience and understanding in the training process is necessary to overcome these natural desires during training.

The cat is a natural and efficient predator, much of whose instinctual behavior is that of a small-size tiger or leopard. To be able to bring down prey, even if that prey is a catnip toy, the cat must be able to lurk, stalk and pounce. Periods of great amounts of sleep will alternate with periods of high activity (hunting). The cat's claws must be very sharp, and eyesight very keen, to be able to spot and kill small prey. The cat displays the hunter's fascination for any small, moving object.

Cats enjoys interaction with other felines and with humans, and the development of extremely close bonds is common, but they hunt and seek out mates alone, not in a pack or pride social structure. This behavior is why the cat is seen as a singularly independent creature.

Mommy and the Litter

Perhaps the first mistake people make when bringing a new kitten home is doing so too early. While conventional wisdom states that it is desirable to obtain a puppy as young as six to eight weeks old, doing the same with a kitten is a mistake that may have lasting negative effects. Not only do kittens benefit from an extended nursing period, they learn much from their mother and littermates that will be beneficial when they do eventually go to their new human family. When at all possible, kittens should be allowed to nurse at will until they are eight weeks old (even though they will likely have been eating solid food for four or more weeks), and should remain with their littermates for at least another two weeks. Responsible breeders normally will not place kittens until even later, after they have completed their kitten immunizations at twelve to fourteen weeks.

The exception to this rule, of course, is when adopting kittens from feral colonies. These kittens have had no interaction with humans, and in fact have learned from their mothers to fear humans. Only the most patient and understanding person can instill trust in a feral kitten after the kitten has passed approximately

three months of age. It is better to remove a kitten from a feral colony as early as five or six weeks of age.

Learning by Example

Kittens learn by example. When they are allowed to observe their mothers, they soon realize that the litter box is the appropriate place for elimination and the scratching post for sharpening claws. If this natural behavior has already developed into a habit before the kitten is removed from her mother, there will be no need for you to try to train your new kitten to develop it. Fastidious by nature, kittens prefer a substance (cat litter) in which they can cover their waste. Owners should be advised, however, that like small children, kittens tend to get very wrapped up in their games and play; this tendency may sometimes cause them to wait until it's too late to make it to the litter box. All "mistakes" should be promptly cleaned so that the place's scent does not make it inviting later on.

Kittens learn by example, but their curious natures lead them to learn by experience, too.

Eager Playmates

Cats are predators, and kittens prepare for the predatory life through rough play with their littermates. Watch a litter of kittens. Just past the toddling stage, they begin to lurk, stalk and pounce, and Momcat will often come running to investigate squeals when the play becomes too rough. This play, during the three- to ten-week-old stages teaches the kitten much about how hard she can bite or scratch before she "hurts," and thus be less likely to inflict damage on her new human "playmates."

Any kitten behavior with people that becomes too rough should never be encouraged, and the kitten should never be rolled onto her back and tickled or "wrestled" with by a human hand. The distinction between play and behavior that calls for true defensiveness can quickly become blurred. Adult cat teeth and claws can do damage to human skin. Rather than striking your kitten or cat when she gets too rough, you should remove your hand, say "no" in a firm voice and turn away from the cat, thus ending the game with clear indication that the cat's behavior was undesirable.

From the Cat's Point of View

When you take your new kitten home for the first time, remember that, first and foremost, the kitten is a baby, and that she has a whole world of exciting new things to explore and learn. Choose a small, kitten-proofed room (a bathroom or a laundry room) that you can set up with litter box, food, water, a bed and toys, and introduce the baby to her room. A nice alternative to this type of room is one of the specially made cat cages available in larger pet-supply stores. They're usually about three feet square and four feet tall, and have a pair of jumping shelves. This is where the kitten should spend her time for the next few weeks, while you are away from home or sleeping. Instead of cruelly confining the kitten, you are giving her her own private den in which she can feel safe, and more importantly, in which she cannot get into mischief! The kitten should be allowed out only when you are home to supervise her activities.

Remember that your home, and everthing in it, provides a constant source of wonder for your cat.

Remember that in your kitten's mind, she *cannot understand why she can do whatever she pleases all day long when you are away from home, only to be chastised when you come home and find the sofa shredded or the Ming vase broken!* She simply cannot make the connection between an activity she did hours ago and the fact that you are now unhappy.

Responding to Unacceptable Behavior

Further, kittens do not respond well to being struck. They appear to make the connection between

performance of an activity, such as jumping onto the kitchen counter, with being smacked; therefore they simply do it when you are not there to hit them!

To train a kitten to follow house rules, there must be an immediate and unpleasant result to doing it, a result that cannot be easily connected to you as its cause. This kind of immediacy can only be accomplished by confining the kitten in an area in which she cannot get into trouble, and letting her out only for supervised play. This same advice will hold true for older cats who may be new to the household, or who may have had a lapse in previous training.

Deter your cat from engaging in dangerous or troublesome behavior with a loud noise.

Years of personal experience has shown that cats can be trained with the use of something as simple as a rolled-up magazine or TV guide. Smacking the magazine smartly on either the palm of your hand, or on the edge of a table, creates a sharp, unpleasant noise that will almost invariably cause the kitten to stop her offending activity. The cat may wait a moment, and then resume the activity. If so, repeat the smacking noise. Eventually, the kitten will stalk off in disgust and look for another activity that will not precipitate this unpleasant noise.

An alternative for more stubborn cases is the by-now tried and true use of water shot from a spray bottle set on fine stream. There are people who also swear by the use of a police whistle.

It seems that in multiple cat households, or even with entire litters, kittens quickly recognize which of them is doing something they shouldn't. Those particular cats will respond to your admonishment while the others will ignore the interruption to their own inoffensive activities.

As the kitten becomes more comfortable with your household rules for cat behavior, she can be allowed out for more and more unsupervised time, and in short order be assimilated as a well-behaved member of the family.

Acceptable Substitutes

In order to aid in the development of this good behavior, though, you must take into account the cat's basic needs and provide acceptable means by which to fulfill those needs. The act of scratching, for instance, is not to sharpen claws, but to help eliminate dead layers of claws. If you do not want your cat to perform this natural activity on your sofa, you must provide her with a suitable alternative—a scratching post. If your cat chews on your houseplant, you can provide her with home-grown grasses for nibbling, as explained in Chapter 5. If the cat is bored, and therefore getting into mischief, you should provide toys and diversions, and even participate in some active games of "tag" or "fetch." Toys can be as simple as an empty paper sack with a wadded piece of paper inside, or a Ping-Pong ball tossed into a bathtub. (Special care should be taken, however, to remove small items that the cat can ingest. Many cat lives have been lost to the simple twist ties that come on loaves of bread, or to needles left on an inviting strand of yarn or thread.)

> **KITTY NO-NO'S**
>
> We are so used to taking aspirin, ibuprofen and acetaminophen when we feel bad that it's tempting to give the same to our pets when they're feeling bad. But no matter how tempted, *NEVER* give your cat these medications. All are toxic to cats, even in one-pill doses. If you suspect your kitten has eaten these or other human medications, or any other kind of poison, call your veterinarian and the National Animal Poison Control Center (800-548-2423).

Declawing—A Frequent Cause of Misbehavior

In many instances, feline misbehavior might have been prevented had the cat's owner not had the cat declawed in lieu of training the cat. Not only is declawing a form of mutilation that should be resorted to only when all other avenues (short of putting the

cat outside to fend for itself) have failed, but it carries with it some potential behavior problems. Cats that are declawed have had their first line of defense removed. As a result, some declawed cats will become biters, after resorting to their next best line of defense.

In other cases, when the surgery is not done exactly correctly, or if the kitten or cat is given litter in her box too soon (veterinarians advise using shredded newspaper in the litter box until the healing is complete), the cat will associate the litter box with pain. As she follows her instinct to dig and to cover, the harsh edges of the litter will hurt. In many cases, a declawed cat will develop a lifelong aversion to a litter box, and will choose inappropriate places for elimination, a choice few owners will tolerate.

Suckling

Another unpleasant feline behavior called "wool sucking" is associated with premature weaning. When the suckling instinct, which not only supplies the kitten with nourishment, but also with comfort and security, is not thoroughly satisfied in early kittenhood, the kitten will look for something else to suckle. This in turn, creates a habitual behavior in which the cat will suck on materials such as wool or cotton, and sometimes even a person's arm or hand. This behavior can potentially last for the duration of the cat's life, but it usually stops once the cat reaches sexual maturity.

Typical Cat Behavior

A well-adjusted, well-behaved cat will sleep much of the time, preferring sunny spots near a window. She will enjoy human companionship and attention, responding by purring and often by kneading her owner with her paws in a rhythmic, alternating action (this, too, is a hold-over from kittenhood, as nursing kittens purr and knead their mothers' stomachs).

The cat's purr is a unique characteristic, and exactly how this sound is produced is still subject to conjecture and controversy. Most researchers believe that the sound emitted is a vibration made when the cat's vocal cords are tensed during the inhalation and exhalation of air. Purring is instinctual, and even two-day-old kittens can make this sound. People have benefited for centuries from the soothing characteristics of the contented cat's purr; the sound is known to reduce blood pressure and heart rate.

A cat's habit of rubbing her face on people or objects is another means of marking territory. A small amount of saliva will be transferred, thus leaving the cat's scent on a favored companion or toy.

Believe it or not, it is possible to train your cat.

Even the best-behaved kitten will display the curiosity for which the cat is well known. Nothing is safe from the bored cat, so ample diversion, provided by toys or, best of all, another cat companion, are the surest way to maintain good behavior. One trait attributed to cats that has not been overstated through history is curiosity. A cat can be fascinated by the most mundane household items and activities, and has the knack for creating games (mostly involving stalk, pounce and "kill") from something as elusive as dust motes flying in a stream of sunshine through the window, to something as tangible as the "dreaded sheet monster" that wiggles under the covers of your bed, usually just before the alarm goes off. Even the most sedate cat will have a driving need to know what is in that sack, what is behind that cupboard door and what is in the very back of that closet.

The Mind-Body Connection

Every cat, whether pedigreed or not, will have a unique personality and temperament. Basic temperament of the cat can be charted on a sliding scale, one that depends quite a bit upon body style. At one end of the

scale are the long, slender cats like the Balinese and the Turkish Angora. These cats are built for motion, and true to their construction, they are active, inquisitive and vocal. They explore their world in a vertical manner. At the other end of the scale are the heavy-boned, short-bodied breeds such as the Persian and the Birman. These cats are sedentary, studious and quiet, and see life in more horizontal planes. Other breeds will fall somewhere in between.

PURRS AND HISSES

Cats make some of the strangest noises; in fact, researchers have documented a range of 16 sounds specific to cats. The two most noticeable are purring and hissing, probably because both are done with gusto.

Purring is normally associated with pleasure, but cats also purr when they're injured or distressed. Purring is a primal response, and kittens start doing it when they're just a few days old. Purring increases in intensity as a cat's pleasure mounts.

What causes purring? When stimulated, the brain sends signals to muscles in the throat and vocal cords to vibrate. It is the action of these muscles that causes the purring sound—and sensation.

Hissing, on the other hand, is a clear signal from the cat to steer clear! It's a sound meant to scare an intruder. In the act of hissing, a jet of air, as well as spit and sound, is shot out through the cat's mouth. The question is, who hissed first, the cat or the snake?

A Special Kind of Intelligence

The intelligence of cats has proven to be quite elusive, defying attempts by pet behaviorists to measure it. However, the observant cat owner has only to watch a cat approaching a problem, carefully designing a solution that will entail the least effort, and carrying out her plan, to know just how intelligent the feline can be.

Cats have a high empathy quotient, and can discern when their owners are depressed, thoughtful or happy. Many cats know that, in a world that has little need for their innate mousing skills anymore, it helps to earn their keep by inventing games that will keep their owners amused. Cats are wonderful actors; they frequently act unexplainably foolish and un-feline, seemingly just for the sake of entertaining their human companions.

Stories abound about the cat's sixth sense—a psychic power that enables them to sense impending dangers. During World War II, many English families depended on the family cat to forewarn them of air raids. In 1980 residents near Mount Saint Helens reported that their cats became agitated and sought shelter in the hours prior to the volcano's eruption. And, of course, there are hundreds of confirmed stories about cats that have journeyed for many miles, succeeding in finding owners who have relocated and left them behind.

Changes in Behavior

Some cats are more shy and reserved and less able to adapt to change than others. When a cat's life is suddenly turned upside down by a move to a new home, an addition to the family (human or pet), a family member leaving the home or any number of other major modifications to the cat's life, the cat can show stress by acting in inappropriate ways. Suddenly, the perfectly litter box–trained cat seeks other places for elimination, or the otherwise quiet and reserved cat becomes more vocal. Cats are even known to actively pout.

Almost any object can become a toy for a curious kitten.

If your cat's behavior makes a sudden left turn, apply your thought processes to what might have caused it, and try to either remedy the situation or offer the cat additional comfort and love. If, however, the behavior has no apparent cause, a trip to the veterinarian may be in order. For instance, a cat who has always used her litter box and then suddenly begins urinating in corners or on furniture may be suffering from a bladder inflammation or infection. An otherwise active cat that begins sleeping an inordinate amount of time, or a cat that suddenly seeks dark places may be feverish or showing the beginnings of an illness. Sudden behavior changes should certainly be checked by your veterinarian for any physical causes.

chapter 10

Things You Can Do with Your Cat

Cats don't normally take to jogging with their owners or catching Frisbees in the park; the cat is, however, a quiet, empathetic companion that can read and respond to his owner's moods. Any cat owner knows that his or her cat is "tuned in" and can offer moments of solace, comfort, mischief and even fun. As mentioned before, it is a known medical fact that a purring cat can lower a person's blood pressure and heart rate, and that people benefit from the act of stroking their cats. Arthritic people keep their fingers more nimble by combing their longhaired cats. Cats are particularly ideal for elderly people and shut-ins, because they don't require their owners to take them out for walks.

Pet Therapy

Numerous programs exist in which cats are taken into hospitals and retirement homes for therapy. If this idea appeals to you, and if your cat is particularly people oriented, you might want to investigate these programs. Your local SPCA or humane society should have information on any local programs for pet-assisted therapy and can give you phone numbers to call. People involved in these programs caution that the pet owner should not independently take it upon him or herself to take a cat into nursing homes or hospitals; there is a liability issue should the cat accidentally injure someone. The established programs offer insurance to cover this contingency. (For more information on this subject, see the book *Volunteering with Your Pet*, by Mary R. Burch, Ph.D., New York: Howell Book House, 1996.)

Next time you take your dog out on a leash, try taking your cat along as well!

There are many touching stories documenting the success of these therapy programs. One large, gentle Maine Coon cat was able to get through to a child who had been comatose for months, simply by lying with the child, purring and gently kneading. Once out of the coma, the child continued to improve with the presence of the cat. Eventually, when the child was allowed to go home, the breeder/owner of the Maine Coon tearfully parted with the cat, knowing that this child, who still faced years of recuperation, needed him most.

Create Your Own Games

Cat owners can enjoy untold hours just watching a playful kitten or a cat stalking invisible prey. You and your cat can invent your own indoor games and set your own rules. Some cats, for instance, are natural

retrievers, and tossing a paper wad or a small foam ball is a frequent source of amusement for both cat and owner. If your cat becomes bored with straight tosses, you can invent variations, such as tossing the toy up or down stairs, or bouncing the ball off walls.

Walking on a Leash

While your cat may not be up for playing a game of croquet, he will undoubtedly investigate the equipment.

Most cats can be trained to walk on a leash, and soft harnesses are made for that purpose. Of course, kittens adapt more quickly, but even old cats can learn new tricks! Begin by allowing the cat to become accustomed to being in the harness. Some react the first time in bizarre ways—some act as though their back is broken, or as if their legs won't work just right. Perseverance pays, though, and most cats will eventually adapt to the harness. Next, try the leash in the house and let the cat lead you. Only gradually begin to assert your guidance.

Only when this hurdle is passed are you prepared to challenge the outside world. Be fully prepared, though, when you do venture out; the outside world can be quite scary to your cat. Sudden noises or motion can cause the cat to take flight in panic, and you should be ready to offer comfort and to put him at ease.

Showing Your Cat

All of the various pedigreed cat registries sponsor cat shows across the country. Classes exist for pedigreed kittens, pedigreed cats in championship, pedigreed cats that have been neutered or spayed and mixed-breed household pets; no matter what cat you own, if the idea of showing him in competition appeals to you, you can do it! Check out any number of monthly cat periodicals for dates and locations of cat shows near you. Perhaps visit one as a spectator to get a better idea of how they are conducted and of what will be expected of you and your cat.

Pedigreed Cats

Pedigreed cats, in all three classes set aside for them, are judged against a written standard of perfection. Because only a small percentage of pedigreed cats meet those exacting standards, the breeder of your cat or another experienced breeder of that breed would be best able to advise you on whether your cat should or should not be shown in these highly competitive pedigreed classes.

Household Pets

The "household pet" category includes all cats, regardless of parentage. The class allows competition by even those pedigreed cats prevented from competition in championship classes because of a disqualifying flaw. In the household pet class, because the cats are judged solely on beauty and condition, and not against a written standard, a pedigreed cat has no particular advantage over the other cats against which he is competing.

Altered Cats

It is quite possible to spend a great deal of money purchasing breeding stock, only to find later that either the hobby doesn't appeal to you as you originally thought it would, or that there is a breed different from your own that you would rather work with. For these and other reasons, it is recommended that beginners start off showing cats in the classification for neutered or spayed pedigreed cats. Called "premiership" in some associations, the "alter class" in others, this category offers the novice exhibitor the opportunity to learn more about the breeds and the lines that make up winning breeds, to hone grooming skills, and to have a great time, all the while making valuable contacts for later breeding-stock purchases. The alter category provides all of the recognition bestowed by

other categories, allowing the exhibitor to earn titles and even national wins!

Breeders frequently charge less for a cat or kitten destined for showing in the alter class and not for breeding. Show cats can be altered for a variety of reasons: Some cats previously shown and titled as whole cats are, for some reason, unable to reproduce; or a breeder could have been "blessed" with too many showable male kittens and not enough people needing to purchase males for stud. Whatever the reason, these cats are available, and can provide a wonderful entrance into the world of cat showing.

Entering a Show

Most cat shows are held on weekends, and are "benched," meaning that all of the cats and their owners must be present at all times during both days of the show. Cats must be entered well in advance of the dates of the show (usually at least two weeks prior) with the entry clerk, who will be listed in the magazine's show schedule. The entry clerk will also have all the information you need regarding fees (an average cat show entry is $35 to $45 for the weekend event), forms to be filled out and motel information for exhibitors coming in from out of town, among other things. Feel free to ask the entry clerk any questions you have. He or she will usually be able to put you in touch with, and bench you with, other breeders of your breed, or with other people showing in the household pet category. This arrangement will help you feel more at home in your first cat show experience.

Showing your cat, whether random-bred or pedigreed, can be quite a rewarding diversion.

For championship or pedigreed alter classes, your cat must be registered with the association sponsoring the show. Kittens of four to eight months of age can normally compete without their registration number, but no wins will be recorded unless the kitten is already registered. This number is issued, along with official registration papers, by the registry when you complete and mail in (with fees) the registration slip given to you by the person from whom you obtained your cat.

Advance Preparation for the Show

Once entered, you will certainly want to go back and reread Chapter 7 on grooming. This will be a beauty contest, after all, so you will want your cat to look as nice as he possibly can. Fleas are *verboten* in cat shows; your cat can be disqualified if they are found, so special care must be taken to eliminate all fleas. A longhaired cat that has been regularly groomed will now have his patience tested. The weeks leading to his debut in the show ring will require diligent attention to the details of grooming. If you have a cat show "mentor" advising you, ask for the special show-grooming techniques applicable to your particular breed, and try them in advance of that final grooming before the show. Claws, both front and rear, are required to be clipped.

If you have already attended a cat show, you know that your cat will be assigned a "benching cage," which will be his home during the show and where he will spend his time between rings. Spectators will stroll the aisles looking at all the cats on display. These benching cages must be covered, and most exhibitors either make or buy specially made show curtains that cover the bottom, top, back and sides of their benching cages. Sizes of these cages may vary, so check with the entry clerk on the size required for this particular show. Some exhibitors go all out, and drape their cages in glitter, glitz and feathers to showcase their cats. Others choose a curtain color that will most complement the color of the cat.

The show's entry information will tell you whether food dishes, litter pans and litter will be furnished by the show, but it's better to be safe than sorry; the best advice is to pack all of these items yourself, along with

your grooming combs, brushes, powders, tissues or a washrag for wiping the cat's face, and any other grooming aids required for your particular cat.

The Big Day Arrives

On the first morning of the show, you will be required to arrive early for "check-in" at the gate. Your cat will be given a preassigned number and you will be directed to your benching cage. Show catalogs, in which you will record your cat's wins, come as part of the entry fee at some shows; other shows require that you purchase them separately. You will then decorate your cage with your curtains, and set up your grooming tools. With longhaired cats, it is wise to do a quick "freshen-up" upon arrival.

The Show Begins

The number assigned to your cat will be announced over the public address system when it is time to bring him to the judging ring. The number of judging rings can vary from as few as four to as many as twelve, depending on the association and on the particular show. This information will be included in your entry flyer. The judging schedule included in your catalog, and attention to numbers being called to the various judging rings, can give you advance notice that your cat will soon be judged.

Each member of your family will have his or her favorite playtime activity to share with your cat.

In advance of that ring call, take your cat out of the benching cage and give him a final grooming once-over. Comb through the cat's fur completely and make sure no tiny mats are lurking. Use a tissue to wipe the eyes and face. Make sure that all claws are clipped. One product that is helpful for most longhaired cats is an antistatic solution, available from pet-supply vendors. Clean cats in the dry atmospheres of show halls tend to develop static electricity in their coats. A light mist of an antistatic spray on the coat and on the comb can help make the cat's hair more manageable.

When your cat's number is called, you are expected to carry him to the appropriate ring. When you arrive, you will find a row of cages behind the judge's table, each marked with a number that will correspond to one of the cats being called for judging. After finding the correct cage, quietly walk in and place your cat in the cage, being sure to latch the cage door. It is inappropriate to address any comments to the judge or to call attention to yourself in any way. Then walk directly out of the ring and take a position with the several other nervous and proud owners, all waiting to see this class of cats be judged.

How Cats Are Judged

Regardless of the registry, all championship cat show judging is done on a pyramid basis. Your cat is first judged in his "color class," then among either males or females and, in some registries, then among cats of the same title (Open, Champion or Grand Champion) as well. For instance, if your cat is a cream Persian, he will first be judged against other cream Persians, and ribbons indicating the judge's ranking of the cats will be hung on the cage. After judging the color class, the judge must then decide on the winners in the breed, or in the case of the Persians, the division. Your cream Persian will then be compared with other Solid Color Division Persians. During this process, your cat, whether in kitten, championship or premiership (alter) classes, will be judged against the written standard that describes perfection in that breed, as well as by how well your cat's competition meets that standard. Ribbons are then hung to indicate the winners of breed or division.

It will be easier for you to understand this process if you have ordered (usually for a very small fee) copies of the association's Show Rules and Show Standards. Each association also has pamphlets that explain both their own judging processes and what the various

ribbons mean, and provide the standard of perfection against which your cat will be judged. Each association has its minor variations and idiosyncracies. Addresses for the associations are listed in Chapter 12.

The judge will go to each cat in turn, and take the cat from the judging cage to his judging table. Your cat will be thoroughly evaluated for conformation, color, coat length and texture and many other factors. While the cat is not required to "perform" in any way, he is expected to be easily handled and not overly frightened or aggressive. (The judges are experts in handling even somewhat testy cats, but prefer that their arms not be shredded by teeth and claws.) Slight nervousness is admissible in cats at their first shows, but most will soon calm down. Many even learn to enjoy the attention and crowds once convinced that the strange person judging them has no intention of pulling their whiskers or having a barbecued cat sandwich for lunch.

Once the color class is judged, the judge or clerk will indicate that each cat may be returned to the benching area. At this time, you should quietly remove your cat and take him back to his benching cage. Having survived your first ring (the cat probably handled it much better than his nervous owner did), it's time to check the show schedule to determine when the next judging will occur.

The Finals

During the course of the day, the kittens and cats from all competitive categories may be called back to the ring for a final. Once the judge has completed the entire competitive class, he or she must now select those cats that best meet their breed standards (in championship) or best represent the beauty and condition desired in a household pet. Normally, ten cats in each competitive category make it to the final, but this number can vary depending on the particular association's rules.

If your cat's number happens to be called for a final, it is perfectly acceptable to get weak in the knees and giddy with excitement. Even the most seasoned exhibitor will be thrilled that the judge has recognized the "obvious" merits in his or her little darling! So put the finishing touches on your cat once again, and proudly carry him to the ring and place him in his cage for his moment of glory!

During the finals, the judge will again take each cat out in turn and present them to the spectators, extolling their virtues and, in general, "showing them off." If your cat wins, a large rosette will be hung on his cage, proclaiming his placement. (Sorry—no money is won.) At the end of the final, you should collect your cat and rosette, then wait your turn to thank the judge.

You will be expected to take your cat with you when you leave at the close of judging on Saturday evening, but may leave your benching decorations intact. The entire process is repeated on Sunday. Then, if you have "caught the bug," like thousands of other cat lovers across the world, you will be scanning the show schedules for the next show near you!

Titles and Awards

Each association offers titles in the championship and altered cat competitive categories, and each has a points-earned system that will be tallied at the end of the show year to determine winners of Regional and National awards. The beauty of showing cats as a hobby is that you can choose and set out to accomplish goals that most suit your limitations in time, energy and money. For some people, the occasional show with a household pet makes for an enjoyable weekend diversion. For others, the opportunity to own and show a pedigreed cat in championship or the alter class for a title or a Regional win is the desired achievement. For still others, the challenge of preserving and showing their favorite breed and achieving the highest awards available means nearly full-time dedication, a substantial expenditure and a heavy travel schedule. Whatever your goal, there is a great deal of enjoyment to be had in sharing weekends with gorgeous felines and their doting owners.

Traveling with Your Cat

Whether you are showing your cat or moving across country, or just would like to have some company on vacation, the cat can be an ideal traveling companion with just a little advance planning and preparation.

Using a Carrier

Your first purchase should be a suitable carrier. If you are traveling by automobile, or if your cat is traveling in the specially pressurized and temperature-controlled part of an airplane's baggage comparment, it will be best to have a sturdy carrier. In fact, airlines have very specific regulations regarding carriers of which you should be aware. Most airlines will allow you to purchase a special pet ticket that will allow you to carry your cat on board with you. If this is your choice, the carrier must be one that will fit under the seat. Regardless of where you decide to carry the cat, you will need to let the airline know in advance that you are traveling with a pet.

A cat carrier is a handy item.

Ideally, your cat will already be well accustomed to his carrier, which should always be used when transporting him to the veterinarian or the groomer. If not, plan to spend at least two weeks getting your cat completely accustomed to being confined. Begin by leaving the open carrier near one of the cat's favorite spots. Put a towel or rug in it, along with one of the cat's favorite toys. You might be pleasantly surprised to walk in and find the cat napping in the carrier, or you might find it necessary to lure the cat in by placing his dinner inside the carrier for a few days. Once the cat has grown accustomed to the sight and feel of the carrier, begin to close him in. Start with brief periods during which you do not move him, and then progress to longer periods during which you walk from one room to another, allowing the cat to become accustomed to the feel of being carried. And finally, take the cat on short car rides in his carrier.

Important Considerations

If your cat feels comfortable in his carrier, there is absolutely no need to even consider tranquilizers, which can leave your cat disoriented and even more frightened!

A cat can manage quite well for several hours without food, water or litter, any of which might spill in the carrier and leave the cat a soggy mess. A longer automobile trip will require stops, during which these can more conveniently be offered—*always with the car doors closed!* Before exiting the car yourself, make sure that the cat is back in his carrier. Searching wooded areas around rest stops (or, worse, dodging traffic in cities) for your frightened escapee could well lead to grief! Even the most laid-back cat, when faced with being loose in a strange environment, will panic and run from you!

Automobile trips in the summer can necessitate additional planning for meals. Health Department regulations require that restaurants not allow pets inside, and the cat cannot be left unattended in a hot car. Temperatures inside a closed vehicle in the sun can soar in a remarkably short time to as much as twenty degrees above the outside temperature, and the cat can suffer heat stroke and even die. Pack

picnic lunches, and take your cat (in his carrier) to a shady spot with you while you have your meal.

Your Cat as a Hotel Guest

It is always a good idea to investigate in advance which hotels and motels will allow pets. (Clubs sponsoring cat shows will provide this information to their exhibitors.) The best-prepared cat owner will purchase a small, fold-down cage for use in hotel rooms for those times when he or she is away from the room, so that the cat cannot escape should the maid come in. If this is not practical, be sure to confine your cat to the bathroom, with a sign posted on the door that the maid should not enter, or put him back into his carrier for the time you will be away.

Make it an unwavering rule, upon entering a new hotel room, and *before your cat is allowed out of his carrier,* to take a few minutes to check the room thoroughly for any hidden dangers or escape routes. Even the best hotels have been known to put mouse or insect bait under beds and behind dressers. Belive it or not, no cat show exhibitor is without at least a couple of stories about their cat getting up into a mattress through a small tear in the bottom. One exhibitor's Burmese cat actually squeezed into a hole in the wall of a hotel room. This situation required that the entire wall be demolished so the owner could retrieve the escapee (at his expense, of course).

And please, please be a courteous guest so that future owners traveling with their cats will not face a "no pets allowed" policy. Take along some plastic garbage bags for disposal of litter and leftover food, and a small whisk broom to tidy up spilled litter. Place a newspaper or a plastic bag under food and water dishes to make sure that none of it is ground into the carpet or creates stains.

part four

Beyond the Basics

chapter 11

Recommended Reading

Books

About Health Care

Carlson, Delbert, D.V.M., and James Griffin, M.D. *Cat Owner's Home Veterinary Handbook* (rev. ed). New York: Howell Book House, 1995.

Hawcroft, Tim, B.V.Sc. (Hons), M.A.C.V.Sc. *First Aid for Cats: The Essential Quick-Reference Guide.* New York: Howell Book House, 1994.

Humphries, Jim, D.V.M. *Dr. Jim's Animal Clinic for Cats: What People Want to Know.* New York: Howell Book House, 1994.

McGinnis, Terri. *Well Cat Book.* New York: Random House, 1993.

Pitcairn, Richard. *Dr. Pitcairn's Guide to Natural Health for Dogs and Cats.* Emmaus, PA: Rodale Press, 1982.

About Cat Shows

Vella, Carolyn M., and John J. McGonagle, Jr. *In the Spotlight.* New York: Howell Book House, 1990.

About Training and Behavior

Bohnenkamp, Gwen (of the Center for Applied Animal Behavior in San Francisco). Cat training/behavior booklets. James & Kenneth

Publishers, 2140 Shattuck Avenue, #2406, Berkeley, CA 94704. (510) 658-8588. Order the following titles from the publisher:

Litterbox Training

Household Destruction

Social Problems

Biting & Scratching

Hyperactivity

Cat Training

Eckstein, Warren and Fay. *How to Get Your Cat to Do What You Want.* New York: Villard Books, 1990.

Fogle, Bruce, D.V.M., M.A.C.V.Sc. *The Cat's Mind: Understanding Your Cat's Behavior.* New York: Howell Book House, 1992.

Johnson, Pam (Feline Behavior Consultant). *Twisted Whiskers: Solving Your Cat's Behavior Problems.* Freedom, CA: The Crossing Press, 1994.

Kunkle, Paul. *How to Toilet Train Your Cat.* New York: Workman Publishers, 1991.

Whiteley, E.H. *Understanding and Training Your Cat or Kitten.* New York: Random House, 1994.

Wright, John C., M.A., Ph.D., and Judy Wright Lashnits. *Is Your Cat Crazy? Behavior Problems and Solutions from the Casebook of a Cat Therapist.* New York: Macmillan, 1994.

About Breeding

Gilbertson, Elaine. *Feline Affair: Guide to Raising and Breeding Purebred Cats.* New York: Alpine Publishing, 1993.

Moore, Anne S. *Breeding Purebred Cats.* Bellevue, MD: Abraxas Publishers, 1981.

General Titles

Alderton, David. *Eyewitness Handbook of Cats.* New York: Dorling Kindersley, 1993.

Becker, Suzy. *All I Need to Know I Learned From My Cat.* New York: Workman Publishing Company, 1990.

Bohnenkamp, Gwen. *From the Cat's Point of View.* San Francisco: Perfect Paws, 1991.

Camuti, Louis. *All My Patients Are Under the Bed: Memoirs of a Cat Doctor.* New York: Fireside Books, 1980.

Caras, Roger A. *A Cat Is Watching: A Look at the Way Cats See Us.* New York: Simon & Schuster, 1989.

Edney. *ASPCA Complete Cat Care Manual.* New York: Houghton Mifflin, 1993.

Fox, Dr. Michael. *Supercat: Raising the Perfect Feline Companion.* New York: Howell Book House, 1990.

———. *Understanding Your Cat.* New York: St. Martin's Press, 1974.

Gebhart, Richard. *The Complete Cat Book.* New York: Howell Book House, 1995.

Hammond, Sean, and Carolyn Usrey. *How to Raise a Sane and Healthy Cat.* New York: Howell Book House, 1994.

Hawcroft, Tim, B.V.Sc. (Hons), M.A.C.V.Sc. *The Howell Book of Cat Care.* New York: Howell Book House, 1991.

Holland, Barbara. *Secrets of the Cat: Its Lore, Legend, and Lives.* New York: Ballentine Books, 1989.

Jankowski, Connie. *Adopting Cats and Kittens.* New York: Howell Book House, 1993.

Kelsey-Wood, Dennis. *Atlas of Cats of the World.* Neptune, NJ: TFH, 1990.

Lawson, Tony, and Pat Lawson. *The Cat-Lover's Cookbook.* Pownal, VT: Storey Communications, 1986.

Mallone, John. *The 125 Most Asked Questions About Cats (And the Answers).* New York: William Morrow and Company, 1992.

Reynolds, Rick and Martha. *Cat Nips.* New York: Berkley Books, 1992.

Shojai, Amy. *The Cat Companion: The History, Culture, and Everyday Life of the Cat.* New York: Mallard Press, 1992.

Siegal, Mordecai, ed. *Cornell Book of Cats.* New York: Villard Books, 1990.

Thomas, Elizabeth Marshall. *Tribe of the Tiger.* New York: Simon & Schuster, 1994.

Wright, Michael, and Sally Walders (eds.). *The Book of the Cat.* New York: Summit Books, 1980.

Magazines, Newsletters and Catalogs

Animal Watch
(published by the ASPCA)
424 East 92nd Street
New York, NY 10128
(212) 876-7700

Cat Fanciers' Almanac
P.O. Box 1005
Manasquan, NJ 08736-1005
(908) 528-9797

Cat Fanciers' Newsletter
304 Hastings
Redlands, CA 92373

Cat Fancy
P.O. Box 6050
Mission Viejo, CA 92690
(714) 855-8822

CATS
P.O. Box 290037
Port Orange, FL 32129
(904)788-2770

Catnip
Newsletter of Tufts University Medical Center
P.O. Box 420014
Palm Coast, FL 32142-0014
(800) 829-0926

Cat World International
P.O. Box 35635
Phoenix, AZ 85069
(602) 995-1822

Just Cats
Box 1831
New Fairfield, CT 06812
(203) 746-6760

Pawprints
P.O. Box 833
North Hollywood, CA 91603

Popular Cats
1115 Broadway
New York, NY 10010

Videos

Kittens to Cats Video
Produced by Pet Avision, Inc.
P.O. Box 102
Morgantown, WV 26507
(800) 822-2988
Order from producer.

Video Catnip (sights and sounds of birds and squirrels)
Produced by Pet Avision, Inc.
Order from producer (address and phone number above).

chapter 12

Resources

Cat Registries

The following organizations perform various functions for their members. Their main function is to register cats and record their lineage. Among other duties, the registries also charter clubs, regulate various aspects of show administration, approve and publish breed standards, recognize new breeds, and put out several publications each year.

American Association of Cat Enthusiasts
P.O. Box 213
Pine Brook, NJ 07058
(610) 916-2079

American Cat Association
8101 Katherine
Panorama City, CA 91402
(818) 781-5656

American Cat Fanciers' Association, Inc.
P.O. Box 203
Point Lookout, MO 65726
(417) 334-5430

Cat Fanciers' Association
P.O. Box 1005
Manasquan, NJ 08736-1005
(908) 528-9797
(The CFA is the largest registry of pedigreed cats in the world.)

Cat Fanciers' Federation, Inc.
P.O. Box 661
Gratis, OH 45330

Happy Household Pet Cat Club
P.O. Box 334
Rome, NY 13442-0334

The International Cat Association
P.O. Box 2684
Harlingen, TX 78551
(210) 428-8046

United Cat Federation
5510 Ptolemy Way
Mira Loma, CA 91752

Humane and Advocacy Groups

Alley Cat Allies
P.O. Box 397
Mount Ranier, MD 20712
(provides assistance for stray cats)

American Humane Association
Animal Protection Division
63 Iverness Drive East
Englewood, CO 80112

American Society for the Prevention of Cruelty to Animals (ASPCA)
424 East 92nd Street
New York, NY 10128
(212) 246-2096

Delta Society
321 Burnett Avenue South, 3rd floor
Renton, WA 98055-2569
(206) 226-7357
(promotes the human-animal bond)

Friends of Cats
15587 Old Highway 80
El Cahor, CA 92021
(619)561-0361

The Fund for Animals
200 West 57th Street
New York, NY 10021
(212) 246-2096

Humane Society of the United States
2100 L Street NW
Washington, DC 20037
(202) 452-1100

I Love Cats
950 Third Avenue, 16th floor
New York, NY 10022-2705
(212) 628-7100

Pets for Patient Progress
P.O. Box 143
Crystal Lake, IL 60039-9143
(815) 455-0990

Pets for People
Call the Animal Shelter in your area, or (314) 982-3028 for information.

POWARS (Pet Owners with AIDS/ARC Resource Service, Inc.)
1674 Broadway, Suite 7A
New York, NY 10019
(212) 246-6307

Sheba Selectacat
3250 East 44th Street
Vernon, CA 90058-0853
(computerized selection process to determine which cat breeds are right for your personality and lifestyle)

Tree House Animal Foundation, Inc.
1212 West Carmen Avenue
Chicago, IL 60640-2999